Getting at the Core

Getting at the Core
Curricular Reform at Harvard

PHYLLIS KELLER

Harvard University Press

Cambridge, Massachusetts, and London, England   1982

Library of Congress Cataloging in Publication Data

Keller, Phyllis, 1930-
Getting at the core.

Includes bibliographical references and index.
1. Harvard University — Curricula.   2. Curriculum
change — Case studies.   1. Title.
LD2129.K44   378′.199′097444   82-6137
ISBN 0-674-35418-4   AACR2

For Robin, Jonathan, and Inez

Preface

Harvard's recent curriculum reform, like so many newsy events of our trendy time, has been widely viewed as a Happening without a Past. It is often taken to be a spur-of-the-moment response to the decline of a common core of knowledge among undergraduates, a riposte by academic conservatives to the Liberty Hall college ambience that is an enduring legacy of the 1960s. The cynics, and there is soundness in their skepticism, see it all as part of the Great Game of Academe: the endless reinvention of the curricular wheel (which, of course, keeps coming full circle), or to change the metaphor, the perpetual shuttle between extremes of prescription and permissiveness.

All this said, the fact remains that the Harvard Core Curriculum is part of a complex and lengthy institutional history of curricular change. That history may be of minimal interest to those who are not close to the school. Nevertheless, it has an important place in the evolution of American higher education and in the relation of higher education to the society at large.

Even its most fervent supporters do not claim that the Core Curriculum represents a sweeping commitment to the wholly new style of undergraduate education. It is neither comprehensive in scope nor radically experimental in character. Indeed, the changes wrought by the faculty affected only a quarter of the Harvard curriculum, the general education component. All other parts were left intact. And what emerged was idiosyncratic in a number of respects; it was not intended as a model for other institutions to follow.

But the fact that a highly visible university succeeded in "doing something" about what many educators and students regarded as the disaster area of undergraduate education in the 1970s made Harvard's reform an event of national interest. How and why it happened is, I think, worth the telling.

Those keen observers of the "patternless multiversity," David Riesman and Gerald Grant, saw little prospect in the 1970s of faculty agreement on even a modest degree of coherence in general education programs (*The Perpetual Dream*, 1978, p. 217). Indeed, the historian of higher education Laurence Veysey argued that the least likely way to improve undergraduate education was to revise the structure of the curriculum. He held that to do so was merely to indulge in petty oscillations between well-worn alternatives, such as greater depth or greater breadth, more elective freedom or more prescription, the proliferation or the restriction of course offerings (see "Stability and Experiment in the American Undergraduate Curriculum," in *Content and Context: Essays in College Education*, edited by Carl Kaysen, 1973).

But the fact remains that American colleges and universities, more than those of any other nation, have devoted themselves to the *ronde* of curricular revision. To understand why this is so is to understand something of central importance to the intellectual character and social role of American higher education.

Curriculum change is the most visible way in which that

institution adapts to changing conditions in our society.
College faculties invest so much of their time and energy in
debate over curricular structure because it provides a useful
framework for discussing issues of a more complex, fundamental, and elusive sort. Here is a familiar battleground—and
a practical vocabulary—for the clash of competing educational
values and ideas, and for striking a workable compromise
among the claims of the academy's internal constituencies. To
properly understand a curriculum reform, one must look not
only at the result but also at why it was initiated in the first
place, at the major issues in contention, at the ways in which
the outcome was achieved, and at what it hoped to accomplish.

When the smoke of debate settled, the features of general
education at Harvard looked strikingly different. But the
Core's greatest significance lay in less tangible measures. To
what extent did it respond to changing social needs and values?
How did it clarify or realign the priorities and purposes of
Harvard College? Is it likely to change the relationship of the
faculty to undergraduate teaching?

Harvard's effort to improve undergraduate education—the
process of getting at the Core—provides rich material for a case
study of the interplay between academic thought and politics.
And however one assesses what came out of it all, the fact remains that a curriculum ultimately is more than a cluster of
courses arranged in an institutionally acceptable pattern. It is
the statement of a faculty, a college, a generation, as to what
they believe to be the character and goals of a college education. So it was with Harvard's Core Curriculum—as with the
century and more of curricular change that preceded it.

I have two kinds of acknowledgments to make: to the reader
and to those who helped me in various ways with the preparation of this book. To the reader I owe some account of my own

role in the campaign for the Core. Trained as an American historian and with a few years of experience in academic administration at another institution, I came to Harvard as an assistant dean in the summer of 1973, two weeks after Henry Rosovsky, who led the campaign, took office as dean of the Faculty of Arts and Sciences.

From that time forward I worked closely with him on the planning and coordination of the effort, serving on several key committees and attending countless meetings. Thus I had the advantage of witnessing most of the events and exchanges recorded here as part of the history of the Core reform. I also had access to private correspondence, internal memoranda, minutes of faculty and Faculty Council meetings, and notes of my own made in the midst of the proceedings or during interviews and conversations with many of the principal participants.

But this book is not in any sense an official or "authorized" account of what happened at Harvard before, during, or after the 1970s. I have tried to make this record of the Core controversies as full and objective as possible and to give a fair and accurate representation of opposing views. The interpretive context, inevitably, is my own.

I have benefited from the valuable advice and criticism of a number of people who read all or parts of this work in manuscript form: in particular, Derek Bok, Hugh Hawkins, Paul Martin, Henry Rosovsky, Dean K. Whitla, Edward T. Wilcox, and James Q. Wilson. I owe a special debt of gratitude to Henry Rosovsky, whose candor, encouragement, and support were constant. Priscilla Kinnear and Ellen Munson voluntarily worked overtime on more than one occasion to aid me with the logistics of manuscript preparation.

But the lion's share of credit for helping me maintain a sense of balance and proportion about issues and events in which I was often intensely engaged must go to my husband, Morton Keller. I cannot imagine that any writer has ever been blessed with—or taken greater advantage of—a more thoughtful reader and gifted editor.

The completion of this book was speeded by a leave of absence, which allowed me to spend several months at Nuffield College, Oxford, during the final stage of writing. That exposure to Oxford provided a most valuable perspective on Harvard. It taught me that educational practices ultimately are shaped by the values of a society, the particular history of an institution, and the characteristics of the teachers, administrators, and students who engage in them. I should be greatly pleased if readers gain as much perspective on their own educational experiences from this account of curricular reform at Harvard.

Contents

1   A Century of Change   1

2   The Search for a Mandate   34

3   Getting at the Core   75

4   The Politics of Curricular Reform   133

Appendix.   A partial listing of Core courses,   167
including only those offered in 1981-82

Notes   189

Index   197

General Education perpetuates itself, if only by seeking
endlessly to discover what it itself is.

—*General Education in a Free Society, 1945*

1
A Century of Change

When Charles William Eliot entered Harvard College in 1849, at the age of fifteen, he and most of his classmates were well prepared for what faced them. They had gone to academies and private preparatory schools closely geared to the Harvard curriculum. And what was that curriculum? Eliot, along with every other student, took thirteen prescribed subjects: Latin, Greek, mathematics, rhetoric, history, chemistry, French, natural history, moral and intellectual philosophy, physics, political economy, constitutional law, and the evidences of natural and revealed religion. After two years of such studies, some concentration was possible, in either foreign languages or mathematics. Students also attended compulsory morning and evening prayers. Classroom recitations and textbooks were the common, almost the only, mode of instruction. Students were graded daily on their preparation, on their classroom performance, on their general behavior.

This was a curriculum and a college life designed not so much to open minds as to fill them—with knowledge and modes of behavior that were fixed, unalterable, not to be questioned. That is not to say there was no interest in expanding the students' mental powers. But the emphasis was on their ability to ingest and retain a prescribed body of information and to think about it in a controlled and logical way. A later time would call this a Puritan mind-set, for want of a better term. Fair enough, if it were not that almost every other American college offered much the same thing.

Appropriately reared or psychologically predisposed students battened on this regimen. Oliver Wendell Holmes, Jr., of the class of 1861, once remarked that he had done a splendid day's work, having completed a dozen tasks—not one of which he enjoyed. Most did not find satisfaction in this manner. Riots, endemic at Harvard and every other American college in the early and mid-nineteenth century, provided a release for high spirits and hostility to the system. At the University of North Carolina a student population of 230 committed 282 rule violations during the single year of 1851.[1]

Harvard College in 1850 was not unlike a modern European secondary school, but it did not bear much resemblance, or even relation, to the vibrant, acquisitive American society that surrounded it. Although Oxford and Cambridge at the time were also removed from their society, they could justify themselves as schooling the children of the gentry in the graces appropriate to their class. No such presumption existed in the United States.

Criticism of this stiff and formalistic education, the sectarianism that was woven into it, and its taint of social exclusiveness rose during the mid-century years. The Massachusetts Legislature in 1850 rebuked Harvard for its failure "to provide practical instruction and student freedom to specialize." And elsewhere American higher education was in a state of ferment. By the 1860s a bold new generation of educational statesmen and institution builders was riding the crest of a reform movement. Francis Wayland installed an elective curriculum and "useful" subjects at Brown in 1850, and enrollments leaped by 40 percent within three years. In 1868 Ezra

Cornell and Andrew Dixon White founded a new university at Ithaca, New York, offering students a variety of ways to realize their career ambitions; its motto was "Any Student, Any Study." Less than a decade later, Daniel Coit Gilman began building the Johns Hopkins University into a citadel of advanced scholarship that rivaled its German counterparts.

Eliot and Lowell: Liberation and Containment of the Curriculum

When Eliot became president of Harvard in 1869, he had a well-developed distaste for what was going on inside—and outside—of the college's classrooms. Indeed, his call for a "new education" in the February 1869 *Atlantic Monthly* materially contributed to his selection as president. With total self-confidence he became the moving force in Harvard's transformation from what often seemed a school for wayward boys into a modern American university. As Oliver Wendell Holmes, Sr., put it, he "turned the whole University over like a flapjack."[2]

Eliot's conviction was that a "real" university would cultivate the individual talents of its students and serve the needs of a dynamic society by dedicating itself to the advancement of knowledge and to the training of experts who could put that knowledge to use.[3] No educational policy could have been more in tune with a nation moving from its agrarian, yeoman, farm-and-small-town past to its industrial, urban, large-organization future. It is not surprising that Eliot's presidency turned out to be one of the most important events in the history of American higher education.

Continental universities, with their strictly professional faculties, were not a useful model, nor were the Ancient Universities of England, devoted as they were to producing the occasional scholar, the dilettante, the amateur, and the semi-civilized aristocrat. What Eliot did was link liberal and graduate education in a distinctive new form: the university college. He devoted his first years as president to raising standards in the professional schools until a bachelor's degree was required for admission, then he turned his energies to reshaping the college. His aim was not to feed students bits and pieces of knowledge but to provide them with an ambience of active, rigorous scholarship, and then—in the full spirit of the individualistic, liberal, laissez-faire nineteenth century—turn them loose to find their own way.

The elective system was his key device. Prescribed studies had imprisoned both faculty and students in a lockstep of teaching and learning. If this were removed, so the theory went, then the faculty would be free to introduce new subjects, offer advanced work, pursue scholarship and scientific research. And students would have the freedom to develop their particular talents and interests.

Eliot did not expect this system to work if it had to deal with virginal minds. He wanted students to get a broad and rigorous exposure to basic academic skills and knowledge in the secondary schools. Stiff entrance requirements would ensure that they were well prepared for Harvard College. Once they were there, free choice, a wide selection of subjects, and an intellectually active faculty would spur them to make bold investments of their mental energy. (Marketplace analogies come readily, and properly, to hand.) If the students made poor choices, these entrepreneurs of the mind, like their counterparts in the market, at least would learn from the experience.

Eliot's elective system was intended to take advantage of individual differences, enlist the productive power of free choice, offer a rich variety of intellectual opportunities, and make it possible for students to explore one area deeply and well. It assumed that all subjects were equally valuable in developing students' mental faculties, that to achieve mastery of one area of knowledge was just as worthwhile as to acquire an acquaintance with many. But Eliot did not equate specialization with narrow professional or technical training. Quality of mind, not expertise, was the initial goal; postgraduate training would take care of the second need for many Harvard students.

Measured by the improvement in quality and stature of Harvard College and its graduate schools, and the relative satisfaction of students and faculty, Eliot's reforms were a smashing success. So, naturally, was Eliot. The average term of nineteenth-century Harvard presidents before him was less than eight years; he held office for forty years, until 1909. The faculty, encouraged (and, increasingly, recruited) to pursue scholarship and research, began to take a more prominent place in the quest for new knowledge and offered an ever-widening range of courses. The college catalogue in 1870 was a four-by-six-inch paperbound pamphlet listing 32 professors and 73 courses; by 1910 it was a five-by-eight-inch cloth-covered book listing 169 professors and 401 courses. The formation of the Graduate School of Arts and Sciences in 1890 signified the high status that scholarship had won at Harvard. Lighter teaching responsibilities and higher salaries added to the incentives attracting able men to university work. And Eliot's insistence on decentralized administration, coupled with the faculty's growing sense of professional identity, strengthened the autonomy of the departments.

Students were no less satisfied; theirs was a freedom of choice unknown to their predecessors. Boyish boisterousness continued, but it did not have the often savage edge of earlier student riots, and the rise of organized sports and fraternal organizations siphoned off much excess energy and self-assertiveness.

Eliot's reforms also changed the college's social goals. Although he did not deprecate learning for its own sake, his major concern was to train an intellectual elite to serve their communities and the nation. He sought to recruit a natural aristocracy of talent—"the brightest boys"—and he was not the least disturbed that this might lead to a mix of social, religious, and ethnic groups. Harvard was far ahead of the other old universities in making room for highly talented Jewish youths: it is hard to imagine Bernard Berenson, '87, the son of an immigrant Lithuanian peddler, at turn-of-the-century Yale or Princeton.

There was a cost to this. Extending college access to students with special talents meant bending entrance standards. Harvard dropped Greek as a requirement for admission (and graduation) in 1887 and treated the remaining standards flexibly. By 1907 about half of the freshman class was insufficiently prepared to meet all entrance requirements. Recognizing the considerable local variation in secondary school programs, Eliot argued against unnecessary barriers that would cut the college off "from a large body of students who have done good work at school, and are perfectly capable of doing good college work."[4] At the same time, his strong interest in the advancement of secondary education stemmed from his hope that public high schools would be able to turn out larger numbers of students well prepared in liberal studies.

As time passed, however, there was more and more evidence of a disquieting gap between the elective ideal and the Harvard reality. Eliot's dogged insistence on liberty and variety met with growing faculty opposition. Some of this was purely reactionary: a hearkening back to the good old days when everyone knew his place in the textbook. But the main thrust of discontent came from critics of the results of curricular do-as-you-please. Eliot counted on students to absorb themselves deeply in subjects that engaged their interests and abilities, but in fact dilettantism flourished. In the early 1900s about a quarter of the student course enrollments were clustered in thirteen massively popular lecture courses taught by pedagogical Barnums commonly known as "bow-wows." Among the illustrious classroom performers were LeBaron Russell Briggs (Rhetoric and Composition); Archibald Cary Coolidge (Medieval and Modern Europe); A. Lawrence Lowell (Constitutional Government); and Nathaniel Shaler (Elementary Geology). Nearly half of the rich array of courses enrolled ten or fewer students. A majority of undergraduates specialized in ferreting out the most elementary courses; 75 percent elected programs without any disciplinary focus.[5] Eliot had assumed a work ethic so universally subscribed to that compulsion was unnecessary. But most students used their freedom to indulge in a variety of interests—social, athletic—firmly rooted outside of the classroom.

The period from 1870 to 1910 saw considerable tinkering with prescription and election in the curricula of liberal arts colleges. New social interests and influences loosened the hold of the classics. Nowhere were the possibilities of individual choice given freer play than at Harvard. Eliot's advocacy left a lasting mark on the segment of American higher education that looked to Eastern colleges and universities for leadership. The power of his case against a uniform curriculum forced even his tradition-minded critics to devise more flexible structures. He may have lost the battle for untrammeled liberty at Harvard, but he won the war to end the lockstep of nineteenth-century American college education.

Eliot's hopes for the development of a public secondary school system that would provide "the brightest boys" with a broad intellectual background were not fulfilled. To be sure, high schools expanded, and their number multiplied to accommodate an ever-rising proportion of the American population. Graduates rose from 2 percent of the seventeen-year-old cohort in 1870 to 9 percent in 1910 and 76 percent in 1970.[6] But the schools were often guided by social interests rather than academic values: by localism, vocationalism, egalitarianism, and by the peculiarly American obsession with "the whole child." Despite the growth of secondary education, what was true at Harvard in 1907 is true today: namely, that stiff college entrance requirements, defined in terms of broad intellectual preparation, run the risk of excluding students who are intellectually able but educationally disadvantaged. There was simply no escaping the inherent contradiction between Eliot's political commitment to liberty and democracy and his educational commitment to high intellectual and academic standards.

In 1904 Barrett Wendell, professor of English, gave voice to traditionalists' discontent with the notion that education should consist of the "study of matters inherently interesting and obviously useful." To organize studies around "what everybody likes best," he scornfully observed, was to accept "the principle of the kindergarten." The widespread adoption of that approach had produced a generation of students who

when they get to college, are flabbier and flabbier in mind. I remember a talk with a Harvard sophomore a few years ago which will illustrate what I mean. He was a pleasantly disposed boy, as as Harvard sophomores are apt to be; and, finding himself unexpectedly aware that his mind lacked cultivation, he did me the honor to inquire how I thought he might best proceed to cultivate it. I answered that the first business should be to take in hand some hard and solid subject, and therewith plough out the traces of kindergarten. The wonder in his big brown eyes lingers with me still. How on earth did I know, he asked, that he had been to a kindergarten at all? I doubt whether I quite succeeded in explaining myself. I had recognized the fact from his inability to keep his attention fixed, for any perceptible length of time, on anything which did not happen to excite his interest; and my explanation appeared not to do so. His culture, I regret to say, seemed little improved when I met him last, about to proceed to our own degree of Bachelor of Arts. The new education had him firmly in its clutches, and the buffets of life had not yet begun to loosen them.

Wendell's own inclination was for "such training as shall enable a man to devote his faculties intently to matters which of themselves do not interest him"; that is, to develop "the power of voluntary, as distinguished from spontaneous, attention."[7]

More restrained critics of Harvard's elective system agreed that free choice fostered neither intellectual seriousness nor high levels of attainment. They sought not only the standards of mental and moral training they identified with the older college but something else as well: a sense of community based on common purposes and values. In 1908, the year before Eliot's retirement, a committee headed by government Professor Abbott Lawrence Lowell called for the abolition of the elective system and its replacement by a combination of broad distribution requirements and a system of majors, which Lowell pointedly called "concentrations."

Drafted to fill Harvard's presidency in 1909, the autocratic Lowell immediately began to install his curricular reforms: a requirement of six full-year courses chosen from three fields outside the area of major study; concentration requirements leading to a comprehensive examination; a tutorial system geared to prepare students for the comprehensive; and academic incentives, in the form of honors degrees, rewarding the achievement of those students who concentrated most effectively.

Eliot's close friend and associate Jerome D. Greene took a dim view of Lowell's concerns: "President Lowell tended to identify the needs of the minority of undergraduates who came from socially privileged families and schools with the needs of Harvard College as a whole." Greene thought that public school graduates were serious and responsible enough to handle the freedom provided by electives. Eliot himself was supposed to have said that after devoting his life "to turning Harvard from a college into a university, Lowell was devoting his to turning it from a university back into a college." But

Harvard historian Samuel Eliot Morison concluded that Lowell "proposed to put back into the academic basket some of the things that had fallen through the mesh during the process of expansion. Of these, the most important was education."[8]

As Eliot's free elective system was in close accord with the values of liberal nineteenth-century America, so Lowell's proposals might be seen as the application of early-twentieth-century progressivism to higher education. His was an effort to adapt traditional values to contemporary realities and by organizational controls to regulate the competing goals of scholarship, utility, and liberal culture. Lowell thought his reforms modified Eliot's work by establishing a necessary balance between liberty and order. As the Harvard philosopher Alfred North Whitehead observed some years later, "Eliot opened the whole field of study for choice, and left it open for quite a while. Finally, in due season, came Lowell, to give it some coordination. He came after about the right interval. What he did was very daring and difficult."[9]

The Fate of General Education in a Free Society

Harvard was hardly a pioneer in the shift from a free elective to a concentration-distribution-elective structure. Through the early and mid-twentieth century that curricular system became and remained the norm for the great majority of American liberal arts colleges. It kept a little of the old prescribed curriculum (though very little: distribution requirements tended to be loose, defined primarily in terms of broad areas of knowledge). At the same time it retained much of the elective system. Students had a quarter or more of their course-taking time at their own disposal and usually had ample freedom within the loose constraints of the distribution and major requirements. And through the major it gave due deference to the rise of departmentally based disciplines.

The Great Curriculum Compromise of the early twentieth century offered something to everybody: the advocates of advanced scholarship, the defenders of liberal culture, the partisans of practical education. But it did not stem the tide of academic specialism. Nor, despite new standards of seriousness, did it provide an increasingly heterogeneous student body with a common learning or shared intellectual purpose. As Frederick Rudolph has observed, the college curriculum remained "a repository of conflicting purposes and contradictory educational philosophies, but a body of standard practices and expectations and a sophisticated bureaucracy imposed a semblance of rationality and sanity on a course of study that was sometimes beyond understanding."[10]

In the years following World War I, Columbia College and later the University of Chicago made heroic and initially successful efforts to give the idea of general education new life.[11] Reacting against the traditions of classical and professional training alike, Columbia was the first to introduce a program of general education for the mix of undergraduates that now included the offspring of New York City's immigrant families (who constituted about 40 percent of entering students at Columbia in the mid-1920s). In 1919 it introduced a required freshman course that surveyed the intellectual traditions of Western society; a decade later a second-year Contemporary Civilization course, emphasizing economics and government, was added. In the 1930s these successes generated a full-blown general education program, including two-year sequences in science and the humanities. By 1936 all students in their first two years studied a common curriculum that sought to provide a comprehensive overview of the main features and significant ideas of Western civilization. The staffing of these courses cut across departmental lines. So strong was the commitment to general education that until 1953 Columbia students were not required to concentrate in a major.

But the pressures of faculty specialization and diverse student interests and preparation undercut the program within five years of its fullest flowering. In 1941 the science faculty withdrew its core course, leaving students the option of selecting departmental courses in any one or a combination of eight fields. By 1969 staffing problems were so acute that only the original course in Contemporary Civilization remained as a program requirement.

General education at the University of Chicago in the 1930s and 1940s was a far more radical experiment. President Robert Maynard Hutchins set the stage in his 1929 inaugural address. It seemed clear to him that universities were quite properly devoted to scholarship and professional training. These functions, he argued, must be kept separate and distinct from undergraduate education. American colleges had a role to play akin to that of European secondary schools: to provide a broad background for the more than 80 percent of students who at that time sought no further educational training. Hutchins proposed that the entire system of schooling be reorganized to combine the last two years of high school and the first two years of college as a single unit devoted to general education.

The curriculum adopted at Chicago in 1937 and fully established in 1942 left no place for electives or majors. It was a wholly prescribed program of interdisciplinary courses in the humanities, social sciences, and natural sciences. These were not survey courses, nor did they rest on the study of a list of "great books," as did the prescribed curriculum at St. John's College in Annapolis. The emphasis was on "the basic organizing principles of knowledge" and on fostering a capacity for sophisticated analysis. Provision was made for well-prepared and mentally swift students to move through the curriculum at a rapid pace. A separate college faculty and comprehensive examinations conducted independently of course instructors rounded out the list of innovations in Chicago's revolutionary scheme.

With some exceptions, most notably during the first years after World War II when an enthusiastic young faculty enlivened things, the Chicago program proved to be impractical. High school juniors were not easily attracted, and graduates found that the Chicago B.A. was not as widely accepted as others. The college became an isolated enclave within the university. Ultimately the inferior status accorded its faculty dampened their ardor and led them to seek opportunities for advancement and graduate teaching elsewhere. The curriculum itself increasingly diverged from the prior training and career interests of teachers and students alike. A basic Introduction to Western Civilization course, added to the Chicago curriculum in 1948, proved to be the most durable element of the undergraduate program. After a brief transition period in the late 1950s, Chicago shifted to a system of disciplinary majors, combined with a mixture of core general education courses and distribution requirement drawing upon offerings of the five collegiate divisions into which the graduate and undergraduate faculties were reorganized.

Despite their significant differences, the Columbia and Chicago programs of general education (together with the Harvard proposals published in 1945) had certain shared values. Their creators were conscious of an obligation to educate students for something beyond vocations and occupations. Whether that something was leadership or citizenship or moral sensibility, it required that students be made aware of the ideas that shaped the society in which they lived. The programs also assumed, in varying degrees, the tasks of transmitting a common intellectual culture or language to a heterogeneous student population and of overcoming the fragmentation of knowledge symbolized and generated by the proliferating academic departments.[12]

The significance of Harvard's *General Education in a Free Society* (1945), subsequently dubbed the "Redbook" for its crimson cover, lay not in its proposed program of college study, but in the philosophy of general education it set forth. The Redbook sought to articulate a "unifying purpose and idea" for American education. Inspired by the patriotism and rededication to democracy stirred by World War II, the authors of the Redbook—predominantly scholars trained in the humanities—defined general education as "that part of a student's whole education which looks first of all to his life as a responsible human being and citizen" in a democratic society.[13]

Besides the war, the massive growth of secondary and higher education influenced their views. Between 1870 and 1940 the population of the United States tripled, but college enrollments went up thirtyfold, and high school enrollments ninetyfold. Forty-nine percent of the seventeen-year-old cohort completed high school in 1940; yet almost three-quarters of them went directly to work. The central question addressed by the Redbook was how to provide school-leavers and college-goers with a "common and binding understanding of the society which they will possess in common."

The answer was general education at every level of schooling. Obviously this could not be limited to a single body of knowledge or a list of great books. Rather, it entailed the transmission of certain mental traits and ways of looking at man that were essential to the conduct of life in a democracy. Free men and responsible citizens needed, above all, "to think effectively, to communicate thought, to make relevant judgments, to discriminate among values." The substantive focus of general education, according to the Redbook authors, should be on *heritage*—study of the past to enrich and clarify the meaning of the present—and on *change*: "the scientific method of thought . . . which demands that you reach conclusions from tested data only, but that, since the data may be enlarged or the conclusions themselves combined with still other conclusions, you must hold them only tentatively." This was a broad but elusive formula. It attempted to reconcile two notions of an educated person: as one fully conscious of a formed by the values and ideas of Western civilization, and as one fully pragmatic in deriving "truth" from experience. The Redbook authors were even less explicit about how their educational ideal might be put into practice: "the ideal of commonness must show itself chiefly in a common reqirement rather than in a common way of carrying it out."[14]

The Redbook's recommendations for Harvard College were somewhat more detailed. It proposed that all students take the same lower-level humanities course (Great Texts in Literature), the same lower-level social science course (Western Thought and Institutions), and one of two lower-level courses in science, emphasizing the historical development as well as the basic principles and methods of physics or biology. These were not to be mere samplings of existing academic fields or to bear any resemblance to introductory departmental courses. Like their Columbia counterparts, they were meant to be interdisciplinary. In addition, students were to take three upper-level courses from a list approved by the Committee on General Education.

What distinguished the general from the special approach to knowledge was a concern for heritage and a focus on broad relationships rather than precise detail: that is, an emphasis on the treatment of subjects rather than the subjects themselves, though the Redbook authors did emphatically prefer the study of "classic" works. Courses in the humanities and social sciences were to stress "the greatest, the most universal, most essential human preoccupations" and the concept of free government—its origin, nature, problems, and risky future.[15]

The Harvard proposals shared with those at Columbia and Chicago the belief in bodies of essential knowledge—information and ideas—that every student should acquire. All assumed that the three major divisions of the curriculum represented distinctive and coherent ways of explaining and evaluating experience. By grouping disciplines in these clusters, general education programs would show the interconnectedness of knowledge and the centrality of method. Each of the proposals stressed as well the need to make students aware of traditions of thought and to confront perennial questions of choice and value. These goals demanded a prescriptive curriculum. But unlike Columbia and Chicago, Harvard made its peace with specialization. It left intact the concentration requirement formulated by President Lowell. However, the actual program approved by the faculty in 1949 broke with earlier conceptions of general education by permitting a limited number of options and alternatives within each area. For Harvard maintained Eliot's belief in the viability of a university college, where the often-conflicting interests of scholarship and education, of individual and communal aspirations could be accommodated. It may well be that the greater flexibility and pragmatism of Harvard's conception of a "unifying purpose and idea" accounted for the widespread influence of *General Education in a Free Society*.

The Redbook marked an important climax in the general education movement. In its search for order, coherence, and continuity with the past, it shared certain values with an older generation of humanists who tried to preserve "liberal culture" from the onslaughts of new subjects, new purposes, new people. But on the eve of social change, which brought near-universal access to higher education, it redefined liberal culture as the heritage of democracy. The authors of the Redbook could not foresee that by the 1970s 60 percent of high school graduates would enter college. However, they did understand the enormous challenge confronting American education in the twentieth century: how to endow the educational system with some common goal and direction while recognizing the diverse needs, interests, and abilities of individuals in a large, complex, and heterogeneous society.

Yet during the twenty-five years after 1945, Harvard's Redbook General Education Program underwent an almost satiric distortion of its objectives. To be sure, neither Columbia nor Chicago (nor other colleges where programs of comparable purpose developed) could maintain a particular schema for very long. But at Harvard the unraveling began immediately. Students were never, in fact, required to take the same humanities, social science and (one of two) natural science courses at the lower level. Instead, "not less than two nor more than four" comparable courses were to be offered in each area.[16] At the upper level, courses approved by the General Education Committee were merely "advisory," leaving students considerable freedom to select departmental offerings for this portion of the requirement. And they made wide use of that freedom. By 1959 festering criticism of Conant's emphasis on the history and philosophy of science came to a head with the passage of legislation permitting students to substitute departmental courses for the lower-level natural science requirement.

An Overseers' Committee to Visit Harvard College in 1961 found disturbing evidence that the program "no longer enjoys the zest, enthusiasm, clarity of purpose, and support it had ten years ago." In 1963 a small faculty committee chaired by Paul Doty, professor of biochemistry, made a valiant but abortive attempt to reformulate the structure and rationale of the program. The committee hoped to remedy perceived deficiencies by introducing a broader range of important subjects (the creative arts, non-Western civilizations, behavioral sciences), a greater emphasis on the methods and findings of contemporary science, more choice and variation in level of difficulty among the elementary courses, and opportunities for sequential learning. But it was ill prepared to cope with the avalanche of faculty criticism that buried every specific proposal to change the structure of requirements. There was a clear majority in favor of the *principle* of general education and broad agreement with the committee's analysis of the program's shortcomings. But in the end the only clear mandate given to the General Education Committee was that it take "a somewhat more venturesome and experimental view of its tasks" and become "quite sensitive to innovation and change" within the framework of the existing program. This was an open invitation to course proliferation, without controlling guidelines.

The upshot was a rapid and dramatic shift away from a common core of courses taken by all students to a minimally prescribed distribution requirement. Between 1963 and 1969 the number of courses sponsored by the committee rose from 55 to 101. These included "innovative and interdisciplinary" offerings such as The Scandinavian Cinema, Computers in Society, and The Health Care Crisis. Such courses were meant to fill lacunae in the curriculum and to examine serious and interesting topics in a program sheltered from the professionalizing influence of departments.

The introduction of courses such as these and of electives negated the central idea of the general education movement. Its sole remaining rationale was the ill-defined ideal of a variety of interesting and worthwhile nondepartmental courses.[17] Lost was the conviction that there was a common intellectual culture—a language spoken by educated men and women—to be acquired through disciplined study of the great intellectual and artistic works of the past.

The Modern Multiversity

By the 1960s American universities had developed beyond Charles W. Eliot's most far-fetched expectations. Clark Kerr held in his 1963 Godkin lectures at Harvard that "the American university is currently undergoing its second great transformation . . . It is being called upon to educate previously unimagined numbers of students; to respond to the expanding claims of national service; to merge its activities with industry as never before; to adapt to and rechannel new intellectual currents." The driving force behind this transformation was a staggering increase in the magnitude, variety, and social importance of knowledge. Kerr grandly predicted: "What the railroads did for the second half of the last century and the automobile for the first half of this century, may be done for the second half of this century by the knowledge industry: that is, to serve as the focal point for national growth. And the university is at the center of the knowledge process."[18]

Responding to an urgent national demand for the increased production and wider distribution of knowledge, universities entered an era of unprecedented growth. Federal support for higher education, primarily earmarked for scientific research, multiplied a hundredfold between 1940 and 1960—when, according to Kerr, it constituted 15 percent of total university budgets and 75 percent of all university research allocations.[19]

At Harvard, government funds accounted for 25 percent of the 1960 budget. The continuing influx of federal funds gave a special cachet to research activity and research productivity, which spread beyond the scientists and engineers who were the intitial beneficiaries. Beginning with the formation of the Russian Research Center in 1948, Harvard social scientists and humanists organized a growing number of research institutes: the Center for Middle Eastern Studies (1954), the East Asian Research Center (1957), the Joint Center for Urban Studies (1959). The creation of these centers also reflected, as former President Nathan Pusey has observed, a surging postwar interest "in international studies of all kinds, in contemporary situations as well as in historical developments, and in exotic languages and places of the world that had earlier been ignored."[20] The effect within the university was a substantially expanded range of intellectual activity. These included new service functions such as the program of Harvard's Center for International Affairs (1958), which brought senior government officials to campus for advanced study, and the work of the Development Advisory Service in providing technical assistance to underdeveloped countries.

An even greater spur to the postwar expansion of higher education was the dramatic increase in the number of college students. Through most of the twentieth century, Americans sought ever-higher levels of educational attainment. Between 1900 and 1955 college enrollments grew more than ten times faster than the college-age population. Between 1940 and 1960 the number of full-time college students rose from 1.5 million to 3.2 million while the size of the eighteen- to twenty-one-year-old cohort declined slightly. The number of colleges increased at the rate of 8 percent per decade. During the 1960s the coming of age of children born in the postwar baby boom enlarged the ranks of college students to 7.1 million (1970), and the number of colleges grew by 27 percent.[21]

Growth in the demand for higher education had two important consequences for American universities. First, many of them were able to adopt increasingly selective admissions policies. At Harvard the size of the applicant pool rose steadily. In 1940 85 percent of 1,234 applicants were admitted; by 1952 the number of applicants had more than doubled (to 3,100), and the proportion admitted had dropped to 63 percent. In 1960 only 30 percent of more than 5,200 applicants gained admission, and the trend toward greater selectivity continued through the next decade (to 20 percent in 1970). Second, as the size of the national college-going population more than doubled between 1960 and 1970, so did the number of faculty positions, and the training of new Ph.D.s to fill these positions took precedence over the other educational activities of the university. Government and foundation funds spurred the growth of graduate programs. At Harvard the number of graduate students increased by 30 percent and the regular faculty by 48 percent during the 1960s, compared with 3 percent for undergraduates.[22]

As research and the training of graduate students (who often worked as research assistants) became the focal activity, the norms of graduate education came to permeate the undergraduate curriculum at many American universities, where quality was measured by the proportion of instruction tailored for actual or potential Ph.D. candidates. What counted in recruiting faculty was the acquisition of scientists and scholars who could staff the burgeoning graduate training programs, attract federal research dollars, and establish a school's reputation as a center of knowledge production.

At Harvard the web of relations between the university and the surrounding society thickened. The growing specialization of the faculty and a deepening commitment to diversity in undergraduate admissions were easily justified as serving national purposes. Charles Eliot's "tireless insistence upon rational individualism, unmitigated diversity, and curricular do-as-you-please" had never been a more apt description of Harvard.[23]

James Bryant Conant had raised funds for a national scholarship program at Harvard in the mid-1930s, but it was not until the 1950s that Harvard actively began to recruit high school students across the nation. A greatly enlarged and highly competitive applicant pool now forced a reconsideration of admissions criteria, which had not been questioned since Lowell's effort to install a Jewish quota in the 1920s.[24] Formal prerequisites for admission in the form of specific secondary school courses were not viewed as a useful filtering device, for the nature of students' prior preparation was no guide to the quality of their college performance.[25] In his 1960 report, Dean of Admissions Wilbur J. Bender posed the crucial question for the college's admissions policy: "Does Harvard want a student body selected solely on the basis of apparent relative academic promise, selected, that is, on a single-factor basis; or are there other considerations, largely nonacademic, which should influence selection, and if so, what are they and how much weight should be placed on them?"[26]

Harvard College admissions officers assumed a continuing commitment to liberal education, defined as "the production of civilized and responsible men and citizens." They made a compelling case against admitting only those students whose academic ability placed them among the top one percent of American college students. Instead, they favored selecting students with a wider range of academic ability in order "to include a variety of personalities, talents, backgrounds and career goals." The issue was not purely philosophical. A host of practical considerations—dominated by Harvard's ambition to be a truly national university and to train leaders who would serve the larger community in every sphere of professional and social life—entered into its final resolution. Nor was the outcome wholly free of anti-intellectual bias (Bender thought that "the top high school student is often, frankly, a pretty dull and bloodless, or peculiar, fellow") or of institutional self-interest (the "Harvard-son group" constituted 20 percent of the college in 1960; reducing this proportion risked losing "the continuing moral and financial support" of Harvard alumni). Dean Bender's own candidly stated prejudice was

for a Harvard College with a certain range and mixture and diversity in its student body—a college with some snobs and some Scandinavian farm boys who skate beautifully and some bright Bronx pre-meds, with some students who care passionately if unwisely (but who knows) about editing the Crimson or beating Yale, or who have an ambition to run a business and make a million, or to get elected to public office, a college in which not all the students have looked on school just as preparation for college, college as preparation for graduate school and graduate school as preparation for they know not what. Won't even our top-one-percent be better men and better scholars for being part of such a college?[27]

Under Bender's leadership, between 1952 and 1960 the profile of Harvard's freshman class significantly changed. The most dramatic alteration came in the variety of the students' geographical background. The proportion from New England, which had declined slowly under Conant, now dropped from 44 percent to 31 percent (with Massachusetts residents sustaining a disproportionate share of the cutback). Student representation from the mid-Atlantic region remained stable at about 28 percent, while all other regions gained, particularly the South, the upper Midwest, and the Pacific states. Harvard also began to recruit black students on a small scale during the Bender years. The new policies did not, however, increase the proportion of students from low-income families. Indeed, at first their percentage declined, as tuition charges rose steadily and the proportion of commuter students fell to 3 percent, compared with over 20 percent before the war. It was not until the mid-1960s that Harvard raised sufficient funds to divorce admissions decisions from the consideration of candidates' financial needs.[28]

The commitment to diversity found expression in other ways as well. Admissions officers developed a high-powered national network of alumni designed to enlarge the pool of applicants. Most of the increase in candidates came from public secondary schools, as the proportion of freshmen from these institutions rose slowly but steadily from 48 percent in 1952 to 56 percent in 1960. On every index of academic ability the quality of incoming classes continually improved, though the most dramatic changes took place at the bottom of each class and at the median. The lowest decile of freshmen in 1960 would have been the 50th percentile of the class entering in 1952. But the proportion of brilliant students did not increase. Even among the most academically gifted candidates, admissions officers looked for those with a "hook"—some personal quality, extraordinary achievement, or status such as geographical origin, school or family tie—to lift them out of the group of comparably qualified candidates. Finally, in 1958 a major shift in financial aid policy guaranteed the continuation of support for all scholarship students who maintained a satisfactory—though not superior—academic record. Bender's view was that "This took us about as far as we could go in removing from the needy student the unhealthy pressures arising from fear of losing scholarship support. It encouraged the scholarship student to plan his college career in terms of basic educational values rather than a grade-getting calculus. And it indicated the Financial Aid Committee's belief that other qualities than those reflected in high Rank List standing were worthy of support."[29]

By 1960 Bender could confidently assert that "the present Harvard student body is much the ablest academically in our history." It was also distinguished by the range of students' prior preparation and the variety of their special interests. This development stimulated a number of faculty-initiated curricular innovations directed at the best-prepared students. A Program of Advanced Standing (1955) permitted those who could demonstrate the completion of college-level work in three or more subjects to enter Harvard as sophomores, thereby skipping over a freshman year largely devoted to general education. The implicit assumption was that these students had already acquired a general education, though in fact their high school advanced-placement courses were most often introductions to a particular major (the highest proportion entered concentrations in mathematics and physics at Harvard).

The original intent of the Advanced Standing Program was to recognize the superior preparation of students from private schools with whom Harvard had historically close ties—Andover, Exeter, Milton, Groton, and others. At the outset, 82 percent of advanced-placement candidates came from private schools. But the intended public message—later enforced by the impact of the Soviet Union's Sputnik—was that schools should offer, and ambitious students undertake, accelerated work. Advanced placement became a national program; by 1961 over 1,000 secondary schools prepared more than 13,000 candidates for advanced placement in more than 600 colleges and universities. Advanced Standing at Harvard came to be a way of singling out and rewarding not the brightest students, but rather those who were unusually well prepared in particular subjects.

In the fall of 1959 Harvard launched a new Freshman Seminar Program. A polar opposite to General Education, the seminars were supposed "to intensify the intellectual experience of the Freshman year" by encouraging students to work closely with faculty members on a particular subject or topic related to the instructor's research interest. As an inducement, the seminars were not graded and there was no formal examination requirement.

Small wonder that the faculty committee reviewing General Education in 1963 asked itself "to what degree are the important educational innovations in the College now going on outside rather than within the framework of the General Education Program?" The next question was "to what degree can these innovations be incorporated within that framework to give it greater strength and resiliency for the years ahead?" They recommended the introduction of new subjects, advanced work, and course sequences that would permit students to develop a particular interest in greater depth. Specialized departmental courses were welcomed as an alternative way of meeting General Education requirements.[30]

Like all reforms, these faculty-initiated changes in the curriculum had some unintended consequences. By 1960 more than half of the students admitted with sophomore standing chose to remain in college for the full four years in order to take graduate courses or complete honors work. The Freshman Seminar Program gained in popularity because of the small size of its classes (and the lack of grades) as well as the opportunity it provided for getting to know a senior faculty member, not simply because it allowed students to share in the teacher's research. And the faculty's effort to loosen up General Education requirements in order to encourage advanced work had as its principal consequence the transformation of the General Education Program into a popular and eclectic repository for nondepartmental courses that catered to a variety of tastes.

In the mid-1960s students themselves began to take the initiative for curricular reform, successfully persuading faculty members to support modifications of existing rules and regulations that would increase options for *all* students. Their logic seemed irrefutable: students had different abilities, ambitions, and energy levels; a standardized curriculum and pace of work created unhealthy pressures that retarded the full development of individual potential; a wider range of options would permit students to find their own most productive level and pace.

In 1958 an option called Independent Studies for Ungraded Credit had been introduced so that departments might permit honors concentrators to engage in study outside the formal course structure. In effect, any department could declare, "This student is of such caliber that if he says he is going to spend one quarter of his time on a useful undertaking he will do so. Give him the credit on faith." By 1967, through student initiative, access to Independent Studies had become so flexible that any faculty member could arrange for any student to do virtually anything under the sun for academic credit. In 1979 the option became a source of campus scandal when a group of students joined together to learn about the football strategy of Harvard coach Joe Restic under the guidance of the team's quarterback, who also received academic credit for his venture into teaching. For most students, Independent Studies became one among a growing number of "wild cards" (options allowing ungraded credit) that could be used to reduce the pace of work and break free of the traditional course pattern.

Piecemeal reforms inevitably threw the entire system of rules and regulations out of whack. For example, seniors had long been excused from the final examination in courses within their concentrations and were allowed to reduce their course load to prepare for general examinations. In the mid-1960s, when most large departments began to eliminate nonhonors comprehensive exams—and sometimes honors comprehensives as well—the rationale but not the practice of senior exemptions disappeared. Reform begat anomaly, which begat further reform, always in the direction of multiplying options and reducing requirements.

The grading system, that quintessential symbol of standardization (and of the ranking of individuals), came under considerable pressure. A group of tutors in the History Department demanded that the senior tutorial be ungraded so that they could teach without the stultifying influence of having to measure student performance. But in the same year they asked that the sophomore tutorial be graded so that students would take it more seriously! The upward trend of grades, which in the 1950s and 1960s was linked to significant improvements in the S.A.T. verbal and mathematics scores of entering students, continued without abatement when these scores began to level off and then to fall after 1963. From 1960 to 1968 the proportion of students earning honor grade averages of B— or better climbed from 41.6 percent to 65.2 percent.[31] Similarly, the proportion of students graduating with honors degrees rose from 39 percent in 1957 to 50 percent in 1960 and 66 percent in 1968.

Grade inflation was scarcely unique to Harvard, and in part it may have reflected a mounting competitiveness among students for admission to graduate and professional schools. But a striking diversity in the norms of evaluation between and within departments revealed the loss of common standards among a highly disparate and specialized faculty. Further evidence appeared in the growing reluctance of members of many departments to judge the qualifications of candidates for faculty appointment in sub-specialties other than their own.

The forces transforming the American university—the knowledge revolution, the rationale of national service, the rapidly expanding student population—effected a series of reforms that, as David Riesman and Gerald Grant have observed, do not "involve a radical reorientation of institutional goals but affect the relations between students and faculty, the process of education, and the context in which it takes places."[32] In essence, two Liberty Halls came into being, one for the faculty and one for the students. In some ways, this was an echo of an earlier time—Eliot's time. But the institutional context of the new cry for greater liberty was significantly different. Eliot had acted against a wholly prescribed curriculum, a narrow range of courses, and a faculty of schoolmasters. But by the 1960s the Harvard catalogue resembled the Boston telephone directory in thickness, its bulk based on the growth of highly specialized courses that attracted very small enrollments. This was the curriculum from which students apparently sought liberation.[33] However, as the loss of control over the standards for its bachelor's degree did not infringe upon the freedom of faculty to teach what they wanted to teach, there was no compelling reason to resist the tide of liberty and equality for all. Fraternity, after all, was an outmoded concept that led to outlandish undergraduate pranks at back water colleges.

In 1963 Clark Kerr classified Harvard as one among a number of new "multiversities":

> What I meant by the word was that the modern university was a "pluralist" institution—pluralistic in several senses: in having several purposes, not one; in having several centers of power, not one; in serving several clienteles, not one. It worshipped no single God; it constituted no single, unified community; it had no discretely defined set of customers. It was marked by many visions of the Good, the True, and the Beautiful, and by many roads to achieve these visions; by power conflicts; by service to many markets and concern for many publics.[34]

The remarkable and celebrated achievements of the multiversity had been won through the encouragement of liberty and diversity. In 1963 it was clear enough to admirers of the new "city of intellect" that the modern university was far from an ivory tower; it was not yet clear how close it was to a Tower of Babel. The chaos unleashed in the campus reign of political activism and cultural radicalism in the late 1960s merely confirmed and heightened trends that already were well under way. In retrospect, it is clear that by the time of Harvard's own siege in April 1969—ironically, the centennial year of Eliot's inaugural address identifying "A Turning Point in Higher Education"—there was no longer a consensus of any sort permitting the orderly governance of the multiversity.

The Breakdown of Order

In the late 1960s, student rebellions occurred in Western European countries and Japan as well as in the United States—countries where the youth cohort was uniquely large, emancipated, and accustomed to the benefits of peace and prosperity. Universities, always gathering places of the privileged and articulate young and almost always (in democratic nations) hospitable to dissident views, provided a natural base for political activists. What seemed incomprehensible at the time was that the universities themselves were the prime object of attack. Students' demands varied in specifics, but everywhere they asserted their right to a new and influential role in university governance and decision making.

The situation was complicated in the United States by military conscription for the unpopular Vietnam war, which gave a special (and personal) justification to rebellion. Political and cultural radicals alike saw the universities as the mainstay and symbol of the status quo. But their ideologies were less potent weapons of mutiny than their militant style and rhetoric: indiscriminate, narcissistic, populist, and morally self-righteous. Malcontents of all ages were drawn to the crusade against the constraints and self-disciplines that limit individual action. What better place to test those limits than in a university committed to free expression and individual autonomy?

The climactic year of Harvard's turmoil was 1968-69. It began with a relatively modest insurrection against faculty authority and university traditions. Two new courses, Social Change in America (Social Relations 148) and Radical Perspectives on Social Change (Social Relations 149) were organized by Students for a Democratic Society. Headed (or fronted) by two junior faculty members, the courses offered a one-sided critical view of American society. They were actually taught in small-group sections by a mix of students: doctoral candidates, undergraduates, and persons "from other sources not easily identified," who effectively controlled the content and grading. Official enrollments rose from 332 in the fall term to 760 in the spring, lending credence to the boast of one SDS leader that the courses played a role in politicizing the student body.[35] Neither the Social Relations Department nor the faculty-wide Committee on Educational Policy could find sufficient grounds to intervene, even after the course became a public scandal, though representatives of the department suggested sheepishly at one point that the course might be more suitably sponsored in the future by the Committee on General Education!

More than two years of intermittent agitation at Harvard finally came to a head on April 9, 1969, when students forcibly occupied University Hall, the main administration building of the Faculty of Arts and Sciences. The ostensible issue was the demand of SDS to abolish Harvard's Reserve Officers Training Corps. Perhaps any issue would have done as well; this one was especially attractive because the faculty, after heated debate, had made several gestures of accommodation, not all of which were supported by the dean, the president, and the Harvard Corporation. Sensing the opportunity for a successful confrontation of "these businessmen on the Corporation who want Harvard to continue producing officers for the Vietnam war or for use against Black rebellions at home," the most mililtant faction of SDS seized the building and evicted administrators from their offices.[36]

Previously the faculty had refused to invoke serious disciplinary penalties for provocative student actions that many believed to be the product of moral passion. The occupation of University Hall precipitated an internal crisis of confidence when President Nathan Pusey, without extensive consultation, called on local police to clear the intruders from the building. Physical force proved necessary to implement the evacuation; 196 people were arrested, and several were injured in police scuffles.

Following the scenario established at Columbia the year before, the police "bust" instantly polarized the campus. Many claimed that the force applied was excessive; others that there had been no need to call in police at all. On April 11, 481 professors met to approve the formation of a special faculty committee to investigate the causes of the crisis and to take jurisdiction over the punishment of student participants. By a vote of 248 to 149 they in effect rebuked the university administration by striking down a resolution declaring that "the overriding moral issue is the initial violent seizure of the building." In a state of demoralization and confusion, the faculty several days later reversed an earlier decision by supporting the plan of militant leaders of the Afro-American students' organization to establish a Black studies department where students and faculty would share responsibility for appointments and curriculum. These startling concessions of faculty authority took place in an atmosphere marked by physical threat, fear, and guilt.[37]

When all was said and done, the events of the late 1960s at Harvard, as at other leading schools, showed that members of the modern multiversity shared no common understanding of its purposes or of the limits they impose on freedom and diversity. They had not, any more than Eliot, found a way to reconcile their political commitment to liberty and democracy with their educational commitment to high intellectual and academic standards. The youth crusaders who set out to repudiate authority chose their target well.

Harvard's transformation during the century from 1869 to 1969 reflected fundamental trends in American higher education. Along with other universities, it became a center of research and scholarship. It trained experts who could apply new knowledge for the benefit of society and extended educational opportunity to an ever-wider circle of young men and (somewhat tardily) women.[38] The era of the 1950s and 1960s saw the fullest flowering—and a number of unimagined consequences —of the ideals of educational liberty and equality, which drew force from the surrounding society. Never before had there been such freedom for faculty and students to pursue their particular interests. But in the process, as in Eliot's day, something important had "fallen through the mesh of the academic basket." That something was what critics of the general education movement called its tacitly political concern with preparing students for their lives as responsible human beings and citizens in a democratic society.

The legacy of the post-World War II decades was an undergraduate curriculum that from one perspective had unparalleled richness and vitality, but from another point of view was an indigestible potpourri reflecting no coherent educational purposes or beliefs. Much the same could be said of the university at large. Each "tub"—school, faculty, students— stood on its own bottom, and not infrequently it stewed in its own juice: disconnected, disaffiliated, anomic.

The turmoil of the late sixties and early seventies extended the creed of Liberty Hall from the curriculum to student life and to university governance at large. Participatory bureaucracy came to be the characteristic form of decision making (and, commonly, nondecision making) at Harvard as in most American universities. But precisely when the university's students and faculty had attained an extraordinary degree of freedom (by past standards), a new discontent began to mount. By the mid-1970s it was clear that there was a growing disposition—often no more than an unfocused yearning—to restore some degree of purpose and coherence to Harvard undergraduate education, to balance liberty with order.

2

The Search for a Mandate

When Derek Bok, former dean of the Harvard Law School, assumed Harvard's presidency in 1971, many advisers urged him to turn his attention to undergraduate education. In his first annual report, Bok observed:

> It would be difficult to point to many substantial innovations in teaching or education that were introduced within the recent past. Changes were made, it is true, but almost all took the form of relaxing old requirements rather than implementing new programs . . . for the most part, the changes are very much the product of a period that has been critical of old traditions and ancient requirements yet largely devoid of new visions for educational reform.

He also noted changes in university governance that limited the capacity of the president to take on the problem directly:

> It has been clear for a long time that the President is neither equipped nor empowered to produce blueprints for educational policy that some forceful presidents were able to draft in the changeful decades surrounding the turn of the century. The President's influence will remain more indirect, centering on his power to appoint deans of the different schools and to participate in the appointments process to insure that faculty selections have been made with the necessary thoroughness and care . . . In the end the President must recognize that the progress of the University will always depend fundamen-

tally upon the imagination and ability of the faculty, students and staff.

But the obligation of presidential influence persisted. Returning to questions of educational policy in his 1972 report, Bok dared to raise potentially divisive curriculum issues in a community still nursing the wounds of uncivil strife. What troubled him was that there seemed to be no "general understanding of what young men and women should expect to gain from a liberal arts education." While laying criticism at no one's door, he concluded that "neither the curriculum nor the formal process of educational development and reform is organized in optimum fashion to further . . . agreed-upon objectives."

Defining the Issues in Undergraduate Education

In 1973 Bok appointed Henry Rosovsky, professor of economics, as dean of the Faculty of Arts and Sciences, the body responsible for all instruction in Harvard and Radcliffe colleges and the Graduate School of Arts and Sciences. Before his appointment Rosovsky had been a prominent figure in faculty affairs. He first publicly expressed his concern about undergraduate education at a faculty meeting in February 1971, when he opposed a proposal to put the General Education Program on an elective basis, arguing that it was impossible to decide the question in the absence of a clear conception of "what the Bachelor's degree as a whole should represent." On that occasion Rosovsky urged that the faculty undertake the "arduous task" of redefining the goals of undergraduate education. A few months later, at Bok's invitation, the two discussed their mutual interest.

Rosovsky was hardly representative of traditional Harvard. A Russian Jew born in Danzig in 1927, he had come to the

United States with his refugee family in 1940. But in many ways he typified the new generation of American scholars who entered academic life in the 1950s. He had attended the College of William and Mary, served in the Army during World War II, and returned to graduate school at Harvard, where he later became a member of the prestigious Society of Fellows. Recalled to military service in the Korean war, he spent a year in Japan, which subsequently shaped his professional interest in Japanese economic history. Rosovsky emerged from graduate school in 1958 as one of a handful of economists with expertise in the Far East and was snapped up by Berkeley to join its growing staff of area specialists with interdisciplinary interests. Within a year he won tenure and was appointed to head the Center for Japanese and Korean Studies.

Rosovsky left Berkeley in 1965, joining the small stream of "White Berkeleyans" who emigrated eastward after the campus confrontations of the Free Speech Movement. At Harvard in the late 1960s he was chairman of the Economics Department and presided over the faculty committee whose recommendations for an academically traditional Program of Afro-American Studies were at first accepted, and then, within a few months, rejected. Disillusioned once again by the politicization and disruptions of university life, Rosovsky steered clear of the faculty caucuses—"liberal" and "conservative"—that negotiated the issues raised in 1969. This lack of identification with any faction made his appointment as dean of faculty politically acceptable.

Toward the end of his first year in office, Rosovsky assembled half a dozen senior faculty and administrators to get their views on the problems of undergraduate education in Harvard College. There followed a series of reports and discussions ranging over many issues. Having exhausted the group's collective wisdom in three or four meetings, Rosovsky called on each participant to advise him on whether he should place the issues before the entire faculty. With one exception, they demurred: educational reform was a fruitless and divisive cause; there was little to be gained and much to be lost by raising large questions in a forum unlikely to provide large answers. But Rosovsky had already made up his mind. In October 1973 he issued a twenty-two-page "Letter to the Faculty on Undergraduate Education." It began with the reminder that faculty membership at Harvard implied not only a special dedication to research and graduate training, but also "a commitment to an old and distinguished tradition of collegiate excellence." That tradition required periodic renewal, but there had not been a full-fledged examination of undergraduate education since the 1940s. His own perspective went back to 1949, when he came to Harvard as a first-year graduate student. Since that time, the size and scope of the faculty had expanded greatly. But he sensed that undergraduates had "not received a fair share of the additions to our intellectual resources." His experience as chairman of a large department and as dean convinced him that many faculty members underestimated the importance of the college to Harvard. It was often the scholars of his own generation—highly specialized, varied in background, having wide experience and associations outside of Harvard—who held the view that undergraduate teaching was "less important and desirable than other time commitments."

In summoning the faculty to a broad review of undergraduate education, Rosovsky also cited other motives, one of which was economic. A clear statement of educational objectives was essential to establish a rational basis for the allocation of scarce financial resources in the years ahead. And as a private institution Harvard could not afford to slight the interests of undergraduates: "The achievements of our faculty in a broad range of advanced research have helped to sustain the high reputation of the College, enabling it to attract what is probably the most gifted and diverse student body in the country. But it is also true that the quality of our faculty is now, as it has always been, significantly dependent upon the resources made available to us by the College and its alumni." At a time when students and their families were increasingly disposed to weigh costs against benefits, it was "not merely a matter of professional standards and institutional pride" to take steps to assure the distinction of a Harvard education.

In addition, Rosovsky confessed to a psychological motive, which proved to be a significant element in his conception of academic leadership: "My purpose is to engage you in a collective effort to identify the major concerns to which we must address ourselves. What may finally emerge from our discussions is perhaps no more important than the fact of deliberation itself, for it is essential that the people who intellectually sustain Harvard College understand the role that they are called upon to play and believe in its importance."

Briefly sketching the important developments that had transformed academic life in the postwar decades, Rosovsky described their centrifugal, atomizing effect on the Harvard Faculty of Arts and Sciences. The number of departments and degree-granting committees had increased by one-third over the last thirty years, and they had "developed varied views of their role within the Faculty." Some saw themselves as primarily, if not exclusively, centers of graduate study; others as major—perhaps overburdened—providers of undergraduate education; still others as "elite and restricted enclaves remote from the general College population." In any case, these academic units were intellectually as well as organizationally isolated from one another. Nor did they commonly take account of educational needs other than those met by their own concentrations.

What was more, the elements that made up Harvard College often appeared to be at odds with one another. Conflicts existed between the interests of General Education and the departments, between the academic program of the college and its extracurricular activities, between the various disciplines, and between the college and the graduate school. Faculty hiring and promotion policy, which ideally sought a balance of abilities, in practice favored research over teaching. Thus incentives and rewards were not congruent with faculty responsibilities. Students also found that their multiple interests—personal development, social life, intellectual growth, vocational identity, political concerns—made it difficult to balance rival claims on their time and energy.

Isolation and competition were fed by laissez-faire attitudes, Rosovsky claimed. Since 1952 the faculty had more than doubled in size, becoming "perhaps uniquely diverse, idiosyncratic and independent." The student population was similarly diversified, although it had grown by a much more modest 14 percent, with similar consequences: "Students no less than faculty have demanded the freedom to pursue their own interests with minimal constraint." Curricular and other reforms reflected this laissez-faire impulse, which contributed to a growing belief that "all constraints are arbitrary, and that all choices are of equal merit."

These pressures and conflicts, he concluded, reduced the interest of the faculty in undergraduate education and blocked their understanding of its purposes. Rosovsky introduced a striking statistic as one measure of change in the postwar decades: between 1952 and 1974 the number of faculty members had grown more than seven times faster than the number of Harvard college students, but the proportion of courses in which undergraduates enrolled had *decreased* by 28 percent. Also, the tutorial program, the sections of large lecture courses, and much of the introductory instruction in mathematics and languages now were staffed to a significant degree by graduate students. The evidence suggested not that faculty members were teaching less, but that there had been a major shift, especially among junior faculty, toward advanced or highly specialized small-group instruction. The greater freedom and status of junior faculty—both highly desirable developments—clearly had had an adverse effect on educational opportunities for the average undergraduate.

Rosovsky held that any change in the curriculum should be guided by some agreed-upon understanding among the faculty of the goals of undergraduate education. He noted that current requirements for the bachelor's degree at Harvard entailed little more than a field of concentration, an undirected sampling of courses in other areas, and minimal training in a foreign language and expository writing. It was not entirely clear what purpose was served by each of these requirements or what broad principles justified them. Was the faculty really satisfied, he asked, with an educational program so lacking in coherence and rationale?

Rosovsky openly admitted that he had not tried in his "Letter to the Faculty" to present a balanced description of education in Harvard College. He dwelt instead on "tensions and inadequacies" because he thought it important for the faculty to "resist the temptation to be satisfied with our successes and achievements." He expected that many would argue, with some justice, "that Harvard College today is better than it has ever been in the past, others that minor improvements are all that is required," but Rosovsky did not agree.

He concluded his letter with a request for individual responses to his statement of concerns. When several hundred replies—mostly letters, some running to a half-dozen typewritten pages—came in, Rosovsky discovered that many faculty members also thought something was amiss. It remained to be seen whether general accord on the need for reform could lead to a new mandate for liberal education.

Determined to engage the largest possible number of people

in a comprehensive study of undergraduate education, Rosovsky decided at the outset not to establish a small blue-ribbon review committee, as Yale and Princeton had done in 1972 and 1973. Instead, in May 1975 he appointed task forces composed of faculty members and students to investigate several separate issues: general education (or, as it was called, the Core Curriculum), concentrations, pedagogical improvement, advising systems, college life, admissions policy, and the allocation of educational resources. Through the academic year 1975-76, these groups organized their inquiries and began to shape their conclusions.[1] But before their findings were released, Rosovsky deliberately set the stage for faculty-wide discussion by drawing attention to the emerging major issues and attempting a broad preliminary formulation of what Harvard's priorities should be.

Published in the fall of 1976, Rosovsky's annual report for 1975-76 was titled "Undergraduate Education: Defining the Issues." Anticipating the conclusions of the task force studying admissions, he began by lauding Harvard's efforts to recruit students with varied social, economic, cultural, and geographical backgrounds. "At a time when it is fashionable to mock the real achievements of American democracy," Rosovsky asserted, "it may be worth stressing that Harvard and other 'elite' institutions transformed themselves as a consequence of deliberate policies." Harvard sought out students in public schools across the nation and raised or diverted huge sums of money to provide financial aid for those who could not meet the high costs of private education. Taking a broad view of individual merit, the college had long since abandoned specific subject matter requirements for admission. As the competition for places in its freshman class intensified in the 1950s and 1960s, Harvard resisted using secondary school grades and S.A.T. scores as exclusive selection criteria. Such a policy would have yielded a group far more suburban, upper-middle-class, and white than the present class, a group intellectually more homogeneous but with a narrower range of qualities and nonacademic talents.

Harvard's outreach for diversity was a remarkable achievement. But Rosovsky thought the college had not effectively confronted one major consequence of its admissions policy: that "our students arrive unevenly—sometimes inadequately—prepared for college work." It was one thing to admit students with weak preparation; it was quite another matter to allow them to graduate with an inadequate education. He recalled that at every Commencement exercise the president of Harvard University ritually welcomed new graduates of the college "to the company of educated men and women." If that phrase meant anything, it surely implied that by the end of their college training every student had achieved a certain level of intellectual development.

Rosovsky then proceeded to describe what he took to be the principal characteristics of that standard:

1. An educated person must be able to think and write clearly and effectively.

2. An educated person should have achieved depth in some field of knowledge. Cumulative learning is an effective way to develop a student's powers of reasoning and analysis, and for our undergraduates this is the principal role of concentrations.

3. An educated person should have a critical appreciation of the ways in which we gain and apply knowledge and understanding of the universe, of society, and of ourselves. Specifically, he or she should have an informed aquaintance with the mathematical and experimental methods of the physical and biological sciences; with the main forms of analysis and the historical and quantitative techniques needed for investigating the workings and development of modern society; with some of the important scholarly, literary, and artistic achievements of the past; and with the major religious and philosophical conceptions of man.

4. An educated person is expected to have some understanding of, and experience in thinking systematically about, moral and ethical problems. It may well be that the most significant quality

in educated persons is the informed judgment which enables them to make discriminating moral choices.

5. An educated person should have good manners and high aesthetic and moral standards. By this I mean the capacity to reject shoddiness in all of its many forms, and to explain and defend one's views effectively and rationally.

6. Finally, an educated American, in the last third of this century, cannot be provincial in the sense of being ignorant of other cultures and other times. It is no longer possible to conduct our lives without reference to the wider world in which we live. A crucial difference between the educated and the uneducated is the extent to which one's life experience is viewed in wider contexts.

Rosovsky expected that the faculty might wish to shorten, lengthen, or alter the list, because professors, as everyone knows, are people who think otherwise. But the real significance of his statement lay in its stress on—indeed, its assumption of—the need to set a minimum standard of intellectual training. The effort to ensure the broadest possible access to college was pointless, Rosovsky thought, if a college diploma did not stand for some level of superior accomplishment. In effect, he pleaded the cause of democractic elitism.

Rosovsky's ideas did not conflict with the educational philosophy of the Redbook of 1945. His educated person was similar in many respects to Conant's citizen in a democracy. But there were important differences in emphasis. Because the views of Conant and his colleagues in the 1940s were colored by fear of totalitarianism and the ebbing of democracy, their greatest stress was placed on preserving the heritage of Western thought. For all its concern in principle about the future, the Redbook in practice was preoccupied with the past.

The social and intellectual atmosphere of the 1970s fostered a concern not with survival but with the quality of life in a democratic society. Rosovsky was part of a self-confident postwar generation of scholars who took the durability of democratic institutions for granted. They had found ample opportunity to develop their talents, had been tested by merit-ocratic standards, and had won recognition almost beyond their expectations. What they feared was not the loss of democracy but its tendency to slide to a lowest common denominator. In a sense, Rosovsky wanted to build quality control into the system of education. Thus his emphasis was on the cultivation of the individual more than on the needs of society. Ironically, he found himself carrying the banner of "personal relevance," the omnipresent educational slogan of the late 1960s, which had been used to justify the study of "what everybody likes best."

Rosovsky admitted that there were problems with his "minimum standard" approach to undergraduate education. It might not be suitable for the one-sided genius—the mathematical wizard or the "born" composer. But such students were rare and their requirements need not be central to a plan designed for the majority of undergraduates. "We should always preserve sufficient flexibility to take care of these very special cases," he argued.

Rosovsky thought critics might also claim that the concept of a *minimum* standard encouraged mediocrity and was remedial in the sense that it tried to make up for the deficiencies of secondary education. They might prefer a national school system on the European model, which assigned general education to the precollege years and reserved higher education for specialized training. But Rosovsky regarded that model as neither feasible nor desirable in the United States. Traditions of local control in American schools worked against national curricular standards. If Harvard were to impose high standards of preparation for admission, it would have no difficulty filling its freshman class. But it would inevitably become more homogeneous, thereby losing the educational value that came from mixing students of diverse talent, background, and perspective, as well as the opportunity to recruit those with brains and talent but an inferior secondary education. He thought that confining general education exclusively to the secondary schools was unsatisfactory in any case, because some subjects, such as economics, did not lend themselves to study at the age of fiteen or sixteen, and others, such as history or literature, acquired significantly different meaning with greater maturity. Furthermore, the value of early specialization for some students was in his experience more than balanced by the value of delayed choice for others. It was in the nature of the American college to offer students the opportunity of a new beginning. He was prepared to view Harvard's task as remedial only in the sense that it should try to make up for its students' lack of a common academic background.

Rosovsky was even less sympathetic to the political argument that standards inevitably imposed conformity, which in turn implied "socializing our students on behalf of this country's 'ruling classes.' " Even if it made sense to talk of ruling classes in America, the standards he proposed "do not represent or preclude any political point of view; indeed, they favor the broadening of sensibilities and the displacement of conventional wisdom by critical thinking." What was more, by setting a minimum standard for all students one made certain that the serious educational disadvantages of some—the product of inferior training—did not persist beyond college graduation.

Finally, Rosovsky addressed himself to the view that education geared to a broad understanding of the contemporary world must inevitably be superficial, that breadth could only be achieved at the price of shallowness. If this were the case, then surely greater depth of study in a very few subjects would be preferable. But Rosovsky argued that "both general and special education can be superficial or profound . . . It is the quality of instruction, not the number of courses, that guards against superficiality." Moreover, breadth could produce its own kind of depth—the deepened insight that came from exposure to a variety of disciplinary perspectives.

So the "problem" of undergraduate education, as Rosovsky came to see it with the help of his colleagues in the task forces, began with the varied qualities of students—their wide range of interests, attitudes, preparation, and talents. The solution would have to be found in a curriculum designed to promote a minimum standard of intellectual development. The effect of Rosovsky's statement of priorities was to turn the spotlight on the issues confronting the Task Force on the Core Curriculum.

A New Look at General Education

The Task Force on the Core Curriculum set to work in May 1975 under the chairmanship of Professor of Government James Q. Wilson. Its charge was to determine what, if any, common learning should be expected of all students, and whether there was any reasonable alternative to a set of college-wide requirements. The Task Force was chosen in part for the variety of its disciplinary perspectives. Besides Wilson, the political scientist, there were two natural scientists, Robert Pound of physics and Leonard Nash of chemistry; Franklin Ford, a historian; Robert Nozick, a philosopher; and Seymour Slive, an art historian. The administration's representative was Phyllis Keller, associate dean of faculty for academic planning. Two students, John Thornton and Nancy Zweng, were selected from a number of applicants because they appeared to be, as Wilson put it, well informed and "reasonably dispassionate."

Rosovsky had originally named Herschel Baker of the English Department as chairman of the Task Force, but ill health had forced Baker to withdraw. When Wilson took over, he tried in vain to recruit another senior literary scholar. Subsequently Slive left the committee to assume the directorship of Harvard's Fogg Museum. The Task Force was to pay a heavy price for these losses; the relatively small representation of humanists was later held against it.

Wilson, a perceptive student of organizational behavior and a brilliant undergraduate teacher, recalls that in the beginning he had no idea where he stood on the issues. Indeed, this was the first time he had ever chaired a committee "without having some notion of where I would like the deliberations to come out." But he did have some clear ideas as to strategy. He was determined "not to begin with a discussion of educational goals." His experience in chairing other faculty committees convinced him that such discussions "will produce either (a) no agreement but much word-snipping or (b) an agreement so abstractly worded as to be either meaningless or educationally unattainable." In part to clarify his own thoughts and in part to identify areas of "natural" agreement, he began by asking each Task Force member to set down his view of an ideal under-graduate education.

The responses stemmed as much from autobiography as from educational theory. Wilson himself had scarcely thought of attending college until he won a debating scholarship to the University of the Redlands in California. He met a weak distri-bution requirement there by taking a minimum amount of work outside of his political science major, and he piled up "an enormous number of government courses." After military service he entered graduate school at the University of Chicago, where he quickly discovered that he had to begin his study of government all over again. Wilson deeply regretted his "premature specialization" and looked back on his college years as an intellectual opportunity that he had not used to full advantage. A proper undergraduate curriculum, he thought, should be more heedful that there was a core of knowledge no educated person should be without—and that students did not know what they did not know.

Franklin Ford's college education at the University of Minnesota was somewhat more balanced than Wilson's: he had had to choose both a major and a minor concentration. But his thinking about the curriculum was colored primarily by his Harvard experience. As dean of faculty during most of the 1960s, he had gained an intimate knowledge of the troubles afflicting the General Education Program and of the disarray that characterized the end of the decade. In 1960 Ford had chaired the faculty committee that endorsed Wilbur Bender's controversial admissions policies. Conscious of the diversity of Harvard's students, he believed in the importance of a "truly shared intellectual experience," a "core that gives undergraduates something in common instead of differentiating them by specialization and by random selection of courses."

Chemistry Professor Leonard Nash came to Harvard College as a scholarship student in 1935. He began to teach at Harvard in 1946 and, caught up in the excitement of the new General Education Program, helped President Conant develop a case history approach to the teaching of natural science. He presided over the resulting course for two decades. A gifted and dedicated teacher, he knew at first hand the difficulties of teaching science to a captive audience of students. He could not imagine any courses that he would require of all students, but he thought it "entirely proper to demand certain skills and capacities of candidates for a Harvard degree." These would have to be carefully defined and tested. Nash was unwilling to assume "that completion of a specified course guarantees possession of a (particular) skill any more than failure to take the course guarantees nonpossession of the skill."

Robert Pound's father was a physicist (and later mathematician) who made his son "aware of physics . . . at an age when few of my contemporaries had even heard of the word." At the University of Buffalo he studied physics and mathematics and sampled a variety of other subjects before his "formal education" was abruptly ended after seven semesters by World War

II. But his views on educational matters were shaped by the "informal education" that began when he went to work in M.I.T.'s wartime radiation laboratory. There he met a number of distinguished scientists, including several from England who stimulated his interest in and admiration of the "Oxbridge" model of intellectual training. Later, as a member of Harvard's Society of Fellows, he enjoyed "continuous contact with a wide spectrum of scholars . . . who developed my appreciation of what other fields than my own involved." This experience of Oxbridge-on-the-Charles persuaded Pound that participation in intellectual life depended first upon acquiring and developing some serious interest. He did not think a convincing case could be made for demanding that all undergraduates acquire a common learning, and he held that both faculty and students were best served by teaching and studying those subjects that engaged their natural interest and enthusiasm.

Philosopher Robert Nozick was then best known for his book *Anarchy, State, and Utopia*, which expounded the philosophy of libertarianism.[2] But his views on undergraduate education were most strongly influenced by the Humanities and Contemporary Civilization program he had gone through as an undergraduate at Columbia College. He held that a required set of courses stressing certain mental skills and bodies of knowledge was essential training for anyone who aspired to intellectual cultivation.

The two students, John Thornton and Nancy Zweng, concentrated respectively in history and anthropology. Both were seniors headed for graduate school. They viewed the existing requirements as arbitrary and were reluctant to increase restraints on student choice. But they were not unsympathetic to the idea of a general education program with "some kind of organizing focus."

After a first exchange of views in the spring of 1975, the Task Force adjourned for a summer of reading and reflection. Returning to a heavy schedule of meetings through the 1975-76 academic year, its members received scores of letters from faculty, students, and alumni, and met with a number of administrators, faculty members, and student organizations. Agreement came slowly and through an intensive exploration of individual preferences about what ought to form the common learning of all students, rather than through a general discussion of educational goals.

But from the first there was virtually unanimous agreement on one point: the existing distribution requirements, which obliged students only to dip more or less at random into the natural sciences, social sciences, and humanities, ought to be abolished. This led naturally to the question whether the Task Force wished to recommend a required Core Curriculum and, if so, how it should be described and how it might be implemented. The phrase "Core Curriculum" came to signify something more broad-gauged than concentration requirements yet more specific than the existing distribution system. Thus the question of the Core was confronted first in terms of structure rather than content: what should be the degree of constraint? rather than, what should it include?

Two Task Force members set the boundaries of the discussion. Nozick wanted a sizable number of specific course requirements; Pound was against nonconcentration requirements of any kind. The others, less fixed in their views, held that the primary purpose of liberal education was intellectual, not vocational; they favored both broad education and exposure to a particular academic specialty. In order to move things along, Wilson pressed his colleagues to cite particular courses, real or imagined, that they considered valuable for all students. It was not yet his purpose, he said, to settle on a particular course content or structure, but only to clarify what they meant when they said they favored a broad education.

The result endorsed neither the Nozick nor the Pound position. Indeed, Pound's critique not only failed to win converts but actually provoked others to defend nonconcentration requirements. A consensus began to fall into place when Nozick professed his willingness to go along with fewer requirements if the machinery for controlling them was strong. And when Nancy Zweng moved from an initial position of skepticism to endorse the emerging Core proposal, a clear student-faculty majority lined up behind four propositions:

1. Certain skills and kinds of knowledge constitute a "minimum standard" of general education for undergraduates.
2. The aims of general education are not compatible with unrestrained choice.
3. Constraints on choice should be sufficiently flexible to take account of the varied interests and capacities of both students and faculty.
4. Flexibility should be contained by agreed-upon educational goals.

By the time of their final report, which Wilson drafted, all of the Task Force members except Pound, who attached a dissenting opinion, had come to favor a Core Curriculum defined by a set of educational purposes rather than by particular courses. They rejected two major alternative views "as being, not trivial, but ultimately unpersuasive." One of these was the free elective curriculum; the other was the view that Harvard should devote more of its energies to preprofessional or specialized training.

The major argument for free choice was that students know their own interests best. Given the diversity of these interests among Harvard students, the case could be made that the university should provide a rich array of courses (as indeed it did) and then encourage students to follow their predilections. But the Task Force was persuaded that "if we are to admit not only dedicated scholars, but athletes, poets, musicians, entrepreneurs, and politicians as well, we cannot expect that all or even many will view the present undifferentiated plethora of courses as primarily an opportunity to seek intellectual growth, or that those who do so will have adequate information as to how to achieve that growth." More students were bewildered than were stimulated by a catalogue with over two thousand courses. While students "cherish their freedom, they also seek guidance, and at present that guidance is not forthcoming from the one group that ought to be an important source of it—the faculty." It was not surprising that "students turn elsewhere for guidance—to roommates, friends, guesswork, or the [*Harvard Crimson*] Confidential Guide." Extensive advising and counseling services were fine in principle, but in practice they were no substitute for a clear faculty policy as to the goals of undergraduate education and the ways in which the curriculum should serve those goals.

But many people warned "that the faculty cannot agree on what studies should be designated as more or less important." The size and diversity of the professoriat, the growth and fragmentation of knowledge, the apparent lack of intellectual community: all of this argued against the practicabililty of a Core Curriculum. Yet having gone through the exercise themselves, most members of the Task Force thought that the faculty's capacity to agree on common requirements should not be prejudged:

> Everything depends on what questions the faculty tries to answer. If it is asked what bodies of knowledge are more or less important, it almost surely will come to no conclusion. There are simply too many facts, too many theories, too many subjects, too many specializations to permit arranging all knowledge into an acceptable hierarchy. But if the faculty is asked instead what intellectual skills, what distinctive ways to thinking, are identifiable and important, it is not clear that either the "knowledge explosion" or the size of the faculty has made that question unanswerable.

A more convincing argument for freedom of choice was that requirements had a cost. If something must be done, something else may not be done, given the constraint of a four-year degree program. A Core Curriculum might well foreclose for many students the development of a minor area of interest and expertise. This was Pound's view. He had a special concern for the unusually talented student who might be forced to forgo advanced work in order to meet general requirements. The other members of the Task Force were sensitive to this problem and agreed that the Core requirement should be held down to the current distribution number of eight semester courses.

The case for greater emphasis on preprofessional or technical education made no converts. The Task Force asserted that "we can do no better than to associate ourselves with the words of John Stuart Mill, uttered on the occasion of his inauguration as rector of Saint Andrews in 1867, adding only 'or women' to references to men":

> Universities are not intended to teach the knowledge required to fit men for some special mode of making their livelihood. Their object is not to make skillful lawyers, or physicians, or engineers, but capable and cultivated human beings. It is very right that there should be Schools of Law and Medicine . . . But these things are not part of what every generation owes to the next, as that on which its civilization and worth will primarily depend . . . Men are men before they are lawyers, or physicians, or merchants, or manufacturers; and if you make them capable and sensible men, they will make themselves capable and sensible lawyers or physicians . . . Men may be competent lawyers without general education, but it depends on general education to make them philosophic lawyers—who demand, and are capable of appreciating, principles, instead of merely cramming their memory with details.

Was the Task Force suggesting that students should have no "consumer rights" in the curriculum? Its members took the view that all colleges need not offer the same "product." Applicants should have a wide range of choices when they set about selecting a college. It followed that Harvard as well as other colleges should supply more information about what they considered to be important in their educational programs, so that students would have a more informed basis for choosing. Admissions officers, too, would have a better basis for matching student and faculty concerns.

Turning next to the shape and content of the Core Curriculum, the Task Force proposed that every undergraduate meet requirements, either by passing one of a small number of comparable courses, or taking an equivalent examination, in each of eight areas: Expository Writing; Mathematical Reasoning and Its Applications; Physical Sciences; Biological Sciences; Western Culture; Nonwestern Civilization and Cultures; Political and Moral Philosophy; and Modern Social Analysis. They composed a provisional statement of objectives for each area, to serve until appropriate faculty committees developed fuller statements of purpose and designed or designated appropriate courses.

The eight requirements added up to a program for fostering skills and conveying basic modes of academic thought, not a program for passing on a received body of information and ideas. Thus Expository Writing self-evidently stressed technique over substance, as did Mathematical Reasoning, which sought to introduce students to the most useful applications of quantitative reasoning. A distinctive way of defining and attaining knowledge was to be stressed in each of the more substantive requirements except for Nonwestern Civilization and Cultures, in which the aim was to increase the general cosmopolitanism of students through learning about cultures other than their own.

The final Task Force report, distributed to faculty and students in January 1977, placed great weight on the design and implementation of a Core program. In this it reflected Wilson's influence on the thinking of his colleagues. Wilson was convinced that unless the faculty organized itself "in ways that engage the continued interest of large numbers of its members in the problems of general or core education, no statement of purpose and no educational philosophy, however cogent or eloquent, will remedy the defect."

Analyzing the practical problems of Harvard's General Education Program, Wilson observed that they had taken two forms. In the early days, through the 1950s, the program was tightly structured: requirements were precise and the number of courses meeting requirements was kept to a strict minimum. Those conditions made it difficult to involve many faculty or to replace those whose interests changed over time. Students often felt that they were forced to study subjects already learned or "utterly remote" from their concerns. But reforms in the early 1960s went to the opposite extreme of too much flexibility. The three very broad categories of requirements—natural science, social science, and humanities—were of undefined intellectual purpose. In the absence of constraining guidelines the number of courses in each category inevitably proliferated and their aims varied widely.

These new conditions made it easier to recruit faculty but increasingly hard to comprehend the rationale of requirements. When the Committee on General Education was instructed in 1965 to sponsor "innovative and interdisciplinary" courses and then in 1970 to allow departmental substitutions for all General Education courses on a two-for-one basis, the entire system collapsed into irrationality. Could anyone understand, much less defend, the implicit assertion that "a course (under Gen. Ed. auspices) on The Films of John Ford is twice as valuable a source of humanistic knowledge as Fine Arts 13, Introduction to Fine Arts, taught under departmental auspices?" Wilson also noted that the proliferation of courses bearing the label Natural Science had come to mean "as any student in science will gleefully testify, that the Nat. Sci. requirement can be met in any number of ways which insure that the student will not learn, or even observe from a safe distance, science."

The Task Force proposals tried to strike a balance between too much structure and too much flexibility by providing for a reasonable number of courses in each of the eight required areas. Flexibililty would be controlled by a full and explicit statement of the educational goals of each category. As a further safeguard against "an inevitable tendency toward course proliferation," Wilson favored an arbitrary limit of eight courses authorized for each area. This would also increase the chance that the courses approved for the Core program would be the best of those proposed. If a committee "must choose the best it must consider carefully what 'best' means, and that in turn requires it to think seriously about the purposes of the requirement and the relationship of the requirement and the course. And when it declines to sponsor a course offering, it need not say that it is a poor idea, but only that it does not serve the purpose of a particular requirement as well as do other proposals."

Finally, Wilson and his colleagues recommended a new administrative structure for the Core Curriculum. Reviewing the difficulties encountered by the existing Committee on General Education, Wilson noted that it was made up of a small group of faculty members whose dedication to the program could not compensate for the fact that they had no power of appointment, no responsibility for developing courses, no explicit guidelines, and no concentration of expertise permitting the evaluation of course proposals. He wanted instead a two-tiered structure: a Standing Committee on the Core Curriculum and eight subcommittees, one for each area, chaired by members of the Standing Committee. The area subcommittees, composed of appropriately knowledgeable faculty members, were to prepare statements fully describing the goals of their areas, identify suitable existing courses, initiate and develop new ones, and advise the Standing

Committee on what resources were essential for the creation and maintenance of Core courses of the highest quality.

The obligation to initiate courses was crucial to Wilson's conception of how a Core Curriculum might be developed, for if the area committees merely responded to course proposals, they would be unable to shape their programs of offerings. The Standing Committee, in turn, was to review, sponsor, and coordinate the development of suitable courses, approve rules governing grading standards and examination procedures, and recommend to the dean of the faculty measures bearing on the allocation of resources and appointments. The area subcommittees would be expected to have the "specialized competence, the continuity in personnel, and the sustained interest" to discharge their curricular responsibilities effectively. In contrast to the many advocates of general education who believe that its fate is tied to the disestablishment of academic departments, Wilson proposed to departmentalize the Core program—that is, to adopt for it the same organizational model that had proved to be so fruitful a source of departmental power and autonomy. Finally, by involving a sizable number of faculty members in the governance of the program, he hoped to elevate its status and make it an integral part of the arts and sciences curriculum.

Replacing the General Education Committee with a new Core structure would leave untended an important residuum of the curriculum: nondepartmental, including interdisciplinary, courses and programs. The Task Force proposed to create a separate Standing Committee on Nondepartmental Instruction to oversee freshman seminars and House courses and to provide a home for worthwhile offerings that were not appropriately sponsored by departments or the Core Curriculum. Thus faculty and student interest in new subjects and approaches to teaching and learning might be encouraged in their own right, without forcing an anomalous linkage to general education or departmental concentrations.

In its concluding pages, the Task Force report turned to the foreign language requirement, "the most conspicuous and specific of the nonconcentration curricular constraints now facing undergraduates." Students could meet the existing requirement by obtaining a score of 560 on the C.E.E.B. achievement test or an equivalent Harvard test. Or they could take one full-year course of instruction in one language—an option cynics described as "serving time." This standard of foreign language study, adopted in 1968, was the low point of a forty-year trend of reducing the number of foreign languages and the level of competence required for the bachelor's degree. Even so, a growing number of students availed themselves of liberal exemption provisions, pleading intellectual incapacity or emotional distress. The University Health Service fostered this process by dignifying the inability to learn a foreign language with a full-fledged medical term: "strephosymbolia."

Taking the view that the current requirement failed to achieve the benefits claimed for foreign language study, the Task Force recommended its abolition. What benefits were claimed? One was that linguistic ability, like all other intellectual skills, was valuable in and of itself. No one took exception to this claim, only to the notion that a fleeting exposure to foreign language study could ensure a meaningful level of mastery. It was asserted, too, that Americans should not be monolingual because it encouraged their isolation in an increasingly interdependent, multilingual world. Again, the Task Force found it difficult to believe that the level of competence signified by a 560 C.E.E.B. score or by a passing grade in one Harvard course produced students with a usuable language skill.

Another argument was that foreign language study provides the intellectual opportunity to break through monolingual and monocultural bonds and to achieve a deeper understanding of the structure of one's own language. The Task Force argued that the existing requirement was unlikely to provide the insight into another society that would come from a course devoted to its history, culture, and thought. And even granting the value of some knowledge of another tongue, "one must still show that exposure to a foreign language is better than alternative ways of using the same time and resources to produce an equivalent gain in one's knowledge of English." On this point the Task Force was inclined to believe that "more time spent on studying and using English would produce more benefits than whatever derivative benefits come from studying French."

The Task Force considered yet another circumstantial argument for retaining the language requirement. It is often said that if American colleges abandoned language requirements, it would have a devastating effect on language study in secondary schools. The Task Force found it difficult to judge this matter, but it was "unwilling to assume that Harvard degree requirements should be determined by reference to the alleged effects its actions will have on school systems across the country, most of which, we imagine, are not as preoccupied with Harvard as we might like to suppose."

The case for abolishing the language requirement rested almost entirely on its inadequacy to meet the goals set for it. The report acknowledged, "Some might argue that what is called for is not the abandonment of the requirement, but its reinvigoration." For the moment, the Task Force members wished only to propose that the educational value deriving from mere exposure to a foreign language was not so great "that, in allocating constraints on the student's scarce time and energy, we should place . . . it on the same level as exposure to the fields we designate as 'core.' "

To some extent the value placed by the Task Force on linguistic skills was reflected in the proposal for a Core expository writing requirement. The rationale for other Core fields rested on the ground that an acquaintance with important ways of thinking about problems produced a gain in understanding "roughly proportional to the effort expended." "We are not convinced," the Task Force said, "that equivalent proportional gains exist in a limited exposure to a foreign language."

The Wilson group deliberately refrained from casting its recommendations in the form of proposals to be voted on by the faculty. It sought only to pose the major issues for discussion and to present the outline of a workable solution. Before going public with the report, Wilson and Rosovsky decided to take some preliminary soundings in late November and December 1976 by discussing it with several small groups of senior faculty from different departments who knew the Harvard scene well, had General Education expierience, and were prospective Core teachers. This selective distribution of the report irritated other faculty members, who thought Wilson was merely lining up support for his proposals. Wilson believed that these meetings substantiated his claim that the report was "a preliminary discussion paper" designed to broaden consultation, not to foreclose it. A set of Core areas had been identified on a tentative basis; they were subject not only to further elaboration but to reorganization and revision.

This approach thoroughly suited Rosovsky's style of leadership. Convinced as he was of the need for reform, he was confident that if he discussed the issues openly and often with a sufficient number of his colleagues, the faculty would find its way to a consensus. Thus in a letter written in January 1977, transmitting the report to all faculty and students, he seized the opportunity to initiate debate by raising a series of specific questions. Picking up on a suggestion made by Wilson, Rosovsky wondered whether the foreign language requirement might not be considered as a separate issue, "perhaps after further review by a specifically constituted committee." Reflecting the privately expressed concerns of many humanists, he questioned whether the proposals might not be improved by making the study of history an explicit requirement and by elaborating on the role of the arts, music, and literature in the area designated as Western Culture. He supposed that a simpler conceptualization of a Core Curriculum might be achieved by combining some fields or perhaps by altering the mixed emphasis on skills, subject matter, and modes of thought. In any case, he invited comments from the entire faculty on the report and on the various questions he had raised.

The Debate over Educational Paternalism

Initial campus reactions to the Wilson report were positive on the whole but sharply qualified. Very few readers took exception to statements reaffirming the value of general education, and none argued with the analysis of what had gone wrong with the existing program. Critics generally clustered in two camps: those who favored the concept and broad outline of a Core Curriculum but objected to details of Wilson's eight-point package, and a smaller group who rejected the proposals either because of principled opposition to nonconcentration requirements or because they thought Wilson's approach was too specific and directive. Each camp included both students and faculty.

Wilson's preliminary soundings led him to expect that a number of scientists would publicly back Pound's stand against general requirements. He also knew that influential figures in some key humanities departments took vigorous exception to the way their fields were represented in the proposed Core program. Indeed, before the Task Force report went into print, Wilson rephrased the Western Culture field requirement to ensure that all students would take at least one course in literature and could choose a second course in literature or in history. With this adjustment he counted on strong support from faculty in the humanities because he believed that the concept of a Core Curriculum was essentially humanistic. But resistance and resentment festered privately in that quarter, although it scarcely surfaced in public.

The nub of the matter was that although the concept of the Core was congenial to many faculty in the humanities, the tone, language, and certain substantive details of the program were not. Influential literary scholars and historians viewed the abolition of the foreign language requirement as insupportable and the omission of a history requirement as a mistake. Many humanists could not discern their own intellectual interests in the broad and vaguely worded statement of educational goals attached to the Task Force description of Western Culture. And they were not happy with the share of requirements apportioned to their fields.

Dissatisfied humanists spoke more openly of their alarm over the Task Force's emphasis on skills and methodologies, which was read as a preoccupation with technique. It was thought that such an emphasis would lead to "cookbook" courses rather than immersion in substantial bodies of literature, history, facts, and theory. Wilson and his Task Force colleagues spent much of their time defending the Core proposal against this view of this intentions.

On the advice of the Faculty Council, the faculty's steering committee, Rosovsky decided to pursue a course of step-by-step diplomacy. He scheduled a series of general faculty meetings to consider the Core during the spring term of 1977. Concurrently the Council, an elected body of sixteen senior and junior faculty drawn from the humanities, social sciences, and natural sciences, with Rosovsky presiding, would consider alternative formulations of the Core areas and make whatever changes seemed constructive and consistent with the intent of the Task Force recommendations. Finally, the Council would test faculty support: not for any detailed set of Core requirements, but for the principle of a mandatory Core Curriculum.

At the first general faculty meeting on February 15, 1977, Wilson introduced the Core report, which attempted to show "how a commitment to general education could be reaffirmed and made more compelling and reasonable." To illustrate both the problem and the nature of the proposed solution, Wilson drew several distinctions between the loose distribution requirement in the General Education Program and the Core's eightfold division. The Core plan covered a greater number of areas and offered a smaller choice of courses. But the most significant difference was that the Core requirement was based on specific educational purposes. Wilson noted that some faculty members, dissatisfied with the status quo, had suggested that the best way to make improvements was to "clean up" or clarify the existing General Education requirement. But in trying to define the purpose of such a requirement, the Task Force had found itself leaning away from the conventional tripartite classification of the curriculum. He readily conceded that the number of areas into which the Core should be divided might not necessarily be the eight provisionally suggested in the report. At the same time it clearly was necessary to develop categories more explicit than natural science, social science, and humanities. Wilson doubted, for example, that any group of professors in the humanities and natural sciences could identify or devise courses "which would guarantee students a knowledge of those vast areas." He further confessed himself "filled with wonder and awe at the prospect of . . . establishing and administering a program in the social sciences such that students taking courses in that section of the catalogue would be assured of having a reasonable and informed acquaintance with the social sciences." The Task Force had concluded that the current distribution requirement, defined in terms of subject areas rather than more particular academic and intellectual purposes, was "not a useful one in assuring either a general education or distribution interest." In effect, it "served only some students' desire to have an opportunity to pursue one or two subjects in great depth."

But it was precisely the lack of specificity characterizing the broad distribution requirement that attracted opposition to the Core proposal. Robert Pound, the lone dissenter on the Wilson Task Force, now reasserted his belief that undergraduate education at Harvard did not need improvement. He was troubled by "the emphasis on 'liberal arts' as an ideal," for in his experience this type of education "has left many students without any serious interest in life or any start on a life work and interest beyond graduation." He saw the imposition of a Core Curriculum as educationally harmful and retrograde. Mandatory courses would reduce the quality of teaching and learning by failing to engage the natural interests and talents of faculty and students; they would inhibit early exploration of concentration choices; they would displace educational flexibility with a rigidly uniform program, and opportunities for advanced work with minimum and inherently superficial standards of learning. Pound thought there were "few subjects whose study did not convey rewards to students," and the issue was "whether or not students ought to be allowed by their own decision to forgo some of those rewards." He insisted that it was improper for the faculty to "legislate educational values for all undergraduates," that Harvard students were clearly able "to make their own educational value judgments."

The ensuing debate dominated faculty meetings in February and March. It had the effect not of moving the faculty to a consensus for or against Wilson's outline of "a workable solution," but of clarifying and elucidating positions on the basic question, what is the aim of general education and how can it be achieved?

Critics of the Core proposal did not necessarily object to nonconcentration requirements or to broad and basic introductory courses introduced either by departments or by faculty committees appointed for that purpose. Nor did they necessarily support greater specialization or a system of free electives. What many objected to was the equation of intellectual breadth with a smattering of knowledge about a lot of different things. They preferred to define breadth as a relatively deep knowledge of more than one subject or discipline. Moreover, they saw no virtue—indeed, they suspected some harm—in general requirements that would bind all students to a common set of studies

George Carrier, professor of applied mathematics, put their case most convincingly. He saw merit in the arguments of both Wilson and Pound. A considerable number of students got an excellent education under existing curricular arrangements at Harvard, yet many did not get the education they needed. He contended that after four years of college study, "students should have been made aware of the variety of intellectual disciplines and subjects within the Faculty of Arts and Sciences, should have at least a rudimentary acquaintance with several of them, a particular interest in a few, and have become immersed in one department or concentration." Since it did not seem possible to achieve all of these desirable goals, the issue to be decided was which among a number of alternative curricular frameworks produced the optimal results. The trouble with the Core proposal, he argued, was that it "precluded the student being able to follow up serious interests, more than at a rudimentary or introductory level, in one or two areas outside of the concentration." Carrier did not think the benefits were worth this cost. The more desirable trade-off was to encourage students to explore in depth a limited set of disciplines "even at the expense of some [greater] breadth in their education." He agreed with Pound that there was no well-defined and generally accepted body of knowledge that all students should possess. On the contrary, there were "many areas of knowledge competing for the attention of students, and it would be a mistake for the Faculty to insist that all Bachelor's candidates finish their college years with an education which is essentially similar."

Core supporters were prepared with counterarguments on every point. They thought that the degree of constraint and "regimentation" inherent in the Core plan was "greatly exaggerated." It would still be possible for a student to major in physics, say, and to study in depth a subject such as classical Chinese. Moreover, there was no reason to believe that the Core requirements would "turn out a uniform educational product." According to Rosovsky, "mere observation was sufficient to establish that the many requirements people encounter in education and in life only rarely turn out a regimented product," and the Core had no such intention. It proposed an orderly framework within which students could make some choices about the subjects they wished to study.

Testimony on the need for such a framework was given by the articulate Nancy Zweng, an authentic former student who had been a member of the Wilson Task Force. Zweng yielded to no one, not even to Pound, in her admiration of the abilities of Harvard undergraduates. But she did not believe one could reasonably leap to the conclusion that the vast majority of students arrived at college with "a focus formed out of concrete interests." On the contrary, she thought that most students "looked at their college years as an opporunity for self-definition, a process which is not helped by being confronted with a catalogue of incredible diversity and an accompanying injunction to choose freely." In her view, the creation of a Core

Curriculum would help students to clarify their interests and to acquire some understanding of those intellectual matters that the more experienced faculty considered important for an educated person.

Professor of Chemistry Frank Westheimer also challenged Pound's contention that students ought to be left free to decide their own curriculum. Under such circumstances, he did not see any reason why the Harvard faculty ought to be asked to confer a Harvard degree. While his own preference was for a more flexible distribution requirement, Westheimer strongly endorsed natural science students "learning something outside of their disciplinary area" and thought it important for students outside the natural sciences to gain "some familiarity with the science and mathematics of the modern world." Since the current science requirement "by general agreement was ridiculously easy to evade," he concluded that the stricter requirement outlined in the Core proposal was distinctly preferable.

Reporting on his discussions with undergraduates, Wilson raised practical objections to Pound's laissez-faire ideal. He noted that students were divided as to a tight or a loose Core Curriculum or General Education requirement. But about one thing they were not divided: even aided by extensive counseling and advising services they felt frustrated, baffled, and overcome by a course catalogue with two thousand entries. The key issue for them was not so much the degree of flexibility as the lack of order and design. The object of the Task Force's recommendations, Wilson argued, "was not to make choices for students, but rather to equip them with the ability to make the choices for themselves."

Core supporters acknowledged that the faculty probably could not agree on a Core Curriculum shaped in terms of subject matter—at least not one that could be squeezed into four years. But they did believe that their colleagues could agree on a Core shaped in terms of various intellectual approaches to knowledge. This was a crucial point, for if the faculty was able to identify a core of necessary skills and ways of thinking, then allowing students to remain ignorant of such important matters would scarcely be worth the potential benefits of uncircumscribed curricular choice.

To true believers in the Core, the alternative suggested by Carrier was the antithesis of general education. One spokesman thought it amounted to the notion that "undergraduates should become pre-professionalized in two areas rather than one." It failed entirely to deal with the problem that while Harvard undergraduates are bright enough, their knowledge is fragmentary. Core enthusiasts expected that the new curriculum would enable students to place their specialized knowledge in a larger intellectual perspective. They also hoped it would remedy students' lack of "a common world of reference." Professor of Government Michael Walzer spoke of the difficulties he encountered in trying to communicate with undergraduates who failed to comprehend even the most commonplace allusions to Biblical stories or major historical events. He saw the Core proposal as an initial step in the direction of having students "study certain disciplines in certain ways so that common references could be established in terms of which rich, complex and allusive conversation could take place on important issues." Walzer supported both the aim of the Task Force and its method of achieving it: that is, having small groups of faculty members commit themselves to articulating what is essential to teach in their own disciplines. Moreover, he viewed the task of subsequent committees as specifying "the standard encounters, books, and issues which one would expect to find among the conventionally recognized and historically ratified paths to knowledge."

In the closing moments of the March faculty discussion, Samuel Beer, professor of government and stalwart of the General Education Program, rose to take the floor. He had been a very junior faculty member when the present program was adopted in the late 1940s. He recalled that he "had understood enough about such matters at the time to recognize that when a faculty discusses something like the rationale of education nothing was likely to happen, since any body, not normally organized into parties, customarily produced a negative majority against every meaningful proposition." He had been surprised and pleased when the program was adopted. Upon reflection, Beer concluded that the proponents of General Education carried the day because they "had managed to discern an educational idea which, particularly in light of the events of the late 30s and 40s, had been trying to emerge." This again, he implied, was a time whose idea had come.

Beer's call for a willing suspension of disbelief effectively rallied support among critics who were dissatisfied with particular aspects of the Wilson proposals and troubled by allegations that the Core Curriculum would prove "rigid and inflexible, a bureaucratic nightmare." The moment was approaching to put to a test the basic issues raised by Wilson's Task Force.

But not so fast. Through the late winter and early spring of 1977, while Wilson doggedly continued to discuss the Core proposal with small groups of faculty members and students, the action shifted to the weekly meetings of the Faculty Council, which Rosovsky dominated. Two wellsprings of disapproval were represented there: scientists of varying ages and a circle of senior humanists nearing the end of lifetime careers at Harvard. And a new figure emerged, Professor of History Bernard Bailyn, first as an outspoken skeptic and critic, then as a craftsman of reconciliation.

Reflecting opposition among the faculty at large to the principle of specific nonconcentration requirements, some scientists on the Council, led by George Carrier, moved to delay further discussion of what those requirements might be. Instead, they wanted to take a direct sounding of faculty sentiment on the fundamental question of curricular flexibility. Did the faculty want "lessened flexibility, along the lines of the Wilson report, or a tightening up and revitalization of General Education," or did the faculty want slightly increased flexibility along the lines indicated by Carrier and others? One scientist even suggested that the main purpose of continuing to discuss the specifics of the Core proposal was to "slide" it in by "getting us accustomed to thinking in terms of the eight-plus field requirements." But neither Rosovsky nor the majority of Council members agreed. They thought Core proponents should have the chance to develop their ideas in a concrete and practical form before testing the underlying principle.

The issues agitating humanists on the Council had more to do with the details of the Core proposal than with the question of requirements per se. These came to focus on what was viewed as the arbitrary nature of the "eight topics" set out in Wilson's report. Several Council members held that a slightly different group of people on the Task Force would have ended up with a different set of topics. Bailyn, who had been a prominent member of the ill-fated Doty Committee that reviewed the General Education Program in the early 1960s, perceived that what was wanted was a more consistent rationale that would give some systematic character to the choice of Core areas. Working from the initial set of topics in the Wilson report, he tried to identify their most general purpose and to recast or redefine "the starting-point areas" in terms of an interrelated set of general principles. Bailyn argued, for example, that the broadest purpose of the Non-Western Cultures requirement proposed by Wilson was to "take the student out of the limitations of his own culture into another way of thinking, another cultural experience. While the more remote the region the better, and the more important the alternative culture the better, the basic effort is to extract the student from his limited environment and give him a broader perspective on the world." Thus it seemed to Bailyn that "the *advanced* study of a non-Anglo-American culture through a real comprehension of its language" ought to be on a par with the proposed introduction to a non-Western culture. So he called for the substitution of a category called Foreign Languages and Cultures, which subsumed both kinds of study and had the added advantage of defusing some of the humanists' resentment of the Task Force position on the foreign language requirement.

Bailyn went on to play the key role in formulating a revised five-area package, which defined the "starting-point areas" of a Core program "according to modes of understanding, approaches to knowledge, hence general principles." Pleased by Bailyn's formulation, and taking into account the general faculty discussions in February and March, the Council turned next to the delicate task of preparing a motion for faculty consideration at the meeting scheduled for May 3, 1977. Meanwhile, Rosovsky convinced Wilson that the changes were mainly "cosmetic," and Wilson joined in the effort that produced the following carefully worded resolution:

That the Faculty endorses the principle of nonconcentration course requirements for the baccalaureate degree, and requests the Dean to appoint committees in the areas listed below. The committees should be charged as follows: (a) to design or designate appropriate courses within these areas; (b) to suggest mechanisms for assuring that such courses will be available in the curriculum; (c) to propose degree requirements within the areas; (d) to report back to the Faculty in the fall term, 1977.

Areas

1. Letters and Arts
   Critical understanding of literature and the arts
2. History
   Public issues in their historical context; historical explanation
3. Social and Philosophical Analysis
   Systematic analysis of social and ethical problems

4. Mathematics and Science
   The vocabulary of science and its use in the study of natural and human phenomena
5. Foreign Languages and Cultures
   Language, and an acquaintance with another language culture

When he introduced the motion to the faculty on behalf of the Faculty Council, Bailyn declared that he saw no need to discuss the general issues further and that he sought only to explain the relationship between the motion and the Task Force proposals. Specific proposals in the motion were clearly different from those in the report, and some of the differences were significant. However, in his view the differences were "less important than the agreement with the general thinking of the Task Force." The Council in fact accepted the Task Force's criticism of the General Education Program; it believed in principle in the value of retaining nonconcentration requirements; it subscribed to the wisdom of the "cautious procedures" outlined in the Task Force report. Unlike the committee that had proposed the General Education Program, the Task Force had not believed itself competent to design a Core Curriculum in detail. It preferred to seek "an endorsement in principle, sketching the merest outline of areas within which a program could evolve."

With all this the Council agreed. Its reservations centered on the definition of the eight specific areas presented by the Task Force. The key changes, said Bailyn, were of emphasis and articulation. The place of history in the Core Curriculum, implicit in the Wilson proposal, was made explicit. The study of letters and arts, as well as history, was no longer confined to Western Culture. And the category of Foreign Cultures had been devised to include not only non-Western but also Western civilizations, where access for many students might be gained through work in foreign languages. The effect of these changes was to replace a topical focus on Western and non-Western cultures with an accent on traditional humanistic modes of inquiry. It was assumed that the existing requirement in expository writing would continue apart from the Core program proper and that the mathematics requirement recommended by the Task Force would be incorporated into the science area. The divisive issue of a separate foreign language requirement was set aside for further study.

In simplifying the original eight-area formulation, the Council had responded to criticism that the selection of Core areas seemed arbitrary, that there were too many elements whose interrelationship was not well articulated. The revised formulation, according to Bailyn, centered "on certain broad, basic modes of understanding: critical, historical, analytical, scientific, and linguistic," rather than on an eclectic mix of topics, skills, and ways of thinking. Recognizing that no division of knowledge "could be absolute, perfect, and convincing to all members of the Faculty," the Council motion was not intended to preclude the possibility of redefining or subdividing the areas. Nor did it suggest that the requirements designed by the committees must be uniform in number and character. These assurances were intended to allay the suspicions of a number of scientists and social scientists who saw in the altered formulation a significant reapportionment of priorities away from their areas and toward the humanities.[3]

Seconding Bailyn's motion, Wilson agreed that the new five-fold formulation was a reasonable and appropriate point of departure. But he cautioned the faculty that a vote in favor was more than an endorsement of the notion of maintaining non-concentration requirements in the curriculum. The real issue was whether or not course choices "should be guided by the Faculty in some fashion." To accept the motion was to reject a general education curriculum in which students took courses outside their concentrations more or less at random.

So the question was sharply posed: did the faculty wish to

set standards of intellectual breadth comparable in specificity to the standards applied in departmental programs? Yet as one wit observed shortly before the question was called, the motion before it was "content-free." What the faculty approved by a resounding voice vote was not a set of statements describing in detail what every student should know, but a set of general principles committing it to depart from more than a decade of educational laissez-faire by reasserting educational paternalism.

But the vote in favor was based also on a widespread understanding that if the faculty did not approve the recommendations of the five new committees charged with specifying degree requirements and designing appropriate courses for the reformulated Core Curriculum, all bets were off. The issue of curricular content thus moved to center stage. And it soon became apparent that conflicting views as to the practical details of education were at least as deeply rooted as differences over curricular policy. Indeed, the experience that followed suggested that perhaps laissez-faire had been less a philosophy of education than a way of living with irreconcilable conflicts.

3

Getting at the Core

The moment of consensus in May 1977 brought to a close the initial phase of curricular reform. Wilson's group had come up with an acceptable solution to the structural problem of redesigning a program of general education. And working from the Task Force initiatives, the Faculty Council had identified a satisfactory starting point for further discussion of substantive details.

The new year was to break into two parts—the first given over primarily to fleshing out the content of the new curriculum, and the second to resolving issues of flexibility that divided advocates of a "hard Core" and a "soft Core."

Working Papers: The Content of the Core

The new formulation of purpose behind the Core Curriculum —that it would foster intellectual breadth by introducing students to the major modes of disciplinary thinking—seemed to be ground on which the interests of faculty and students might coincide. And as long as the aims of the new program were broadly defined, and its means unspecified, faculty differences of opinion remained muted. Indeed, physicist Robert

Pound complained more than once that it was impossible to attack so blurred and elusive a target. Just so.

From the administration's point of view, the coming academic year, 1977-78, promised to be one long marathon negotiating session. Rosovsky believed that further faculty consensus was essential for serious reform. He was prepared, as the Core proposal acquired detail, to hear the views of every member of the faculty, if necessary. He began to introduce himself on public occasions as "Iron Pants," borrowing the nickname bestowed on Soviet Foreign Minister Molotov for his ability to outlast every other participant in committee meetings. As for the frequency of meetings, what had gone before seemed modest by comparison.

In order not to lose momentum after the May 1977 vote, Rosovsky immediately appointed two senior faculty members from different departments to work, during the summer, on each of the five proposed areas: Professors John L. Clive (history) and Walter J. Kaiser (English and comparative literature) in Letters and Arts; Professors Bernard Bailyn (history) and Stanley H. Hoffmann (government) in History; Professors Dwight H. Perkins (economics) and Michael L. Walzer (government) in Social and Philosophical Analysis; Professors John E. Dowling (biology) and Harvey Brooks (applied sciences) in Mathematics and Science; Professors Donald L. Fanger (Slavic languages and literature) and Edwin O. Reischauer (East Asian languages and civilizations) in Foreign Languages and Cultures. Each pair was asked to explore alternative definitions of their area, to clarify the viable choices, and to propose priorities. They were asked also to consider the relationship between their area and the others, and to consult colleagues about new and existing course prospects. It was a large and improbable menu for summer digestion. By September the several pairs had been able to do no more than identify the intellectual and pedagogical issues within their purview and shape independent proposals in the form of rough working papers. Though it was not his original intention, the indefatigable Rosovsky decided to draw these groups together into a central planning committee under his direction to review and criticize each others' work, determine the relative weight assigned to each area, and devise an integrated curriculum.

The following sections describe the central committee's recommendations in each area, the considerations on which they were based, and some of the main objections posed by critics. While the substantive issues naturally differ from area to area, the obstacles to agreement were strikingly similar in one respect. Even within a seemingly coherent field of study, scholars set themelves different tasks and employ or emphasize different tools of inquiry. So even among professionally homogeneous groups of consultants, the problem remained one of determining what should be basic to general education.

Literature and Arts

What college-wide requirements made sense in Literature and Arts? As in all Core areas, certain conditions had to be met. The number of requirements must be kept to a minimum, and they must permit students some degree of choice among courses. The objective, broadly stated, was to help students acquire a working knowledge of important ways of thinking and related intellectual skills. In this area the aim was to foster a "critical understanding of literature and the arts."

These constraints ruled out chronological or systematic survey courses in which the primary emphasis is on mapping out a field of study. To the Core planners it seemed best to begin by focusing on what students should be expected to gain from courses in this area, namely, the ability to comprehend and respond to works of art. At the very least, this demanded well-developed skills of reading, seeing, and hearing. Students also would need to be aware of the possibilities and limitations of the artist's chosen medium and the means available for expression; to observe the relationship between form and content; to understand the interplay among individual talent, artistic tradition, and historical context; to perceive, in sum, how artists contrive statements about aspects of human nature and experience.

But, the Core planners hastened to add, it is "as important for students to learn *what* men have thought about their experience as *how* they have expressed and communicated those thoughts." They insisted that Core courses introduce students to a few great classics of literature, art, architecture, and music —works unrivaled for their subtlety of thought, sophistication of expression, and enduring significance. Skills of perception and analysis were to be taught through exposure to a coherently ordered body of such masterworks. Two further principles guided their proposals: first, that written work should take precedence over other forms of artistic expression and second, that only certain arts and art forms in literature, music, and the visual arts were appropriate for the Core program.

The argument behind the first principle was simply that verbal forms of expression have always been dominant in our culture and continue to be the chief mode of human communication. What this stricture meant in practice was that the study of literature would be considered mandatory and that students could choose between course work in music and in fine arts. The second guiding principle was that Core courses should be based on the study of works drawn from major traditions. This was not intended to deny the value of studying such arts as film, the folk tale, ethnic music, and decorative arts, nor the ability of truly gifted teachers to transform any subject "into an intellectually far-reaching study." But limits had to be set, and "although one may indeed be able to perceive eternity in a grain of sand, it is at least easier to begin with the great mountain ranges." Further, channeling all undergraduates through a relatively narrow range of courses would increase the likelihood of shared intellectual experiences.

Getting down to specifics, the Literature and Arts Core planners recommended three semester-course requirements: one in literature, one in fine arts or music, and one in a subdivision called "contexts of culture," which would contain courses "based upon a synoptic fusion of several disciplines."

Course A: Literature   After examining various alternatives, the planners concluded that the most promising way to achieve their aims was to organize literature courses around the examination of major texts in a specific genre. But these courses were not intended to be simply studies of the historical development or structural characteristics of a particular literary form:

> What lies behind the vision of comedy or the vision of tragedy? What are the aspirations that inform the world of epic or the world of romance? What attitudes are inherent in the pastoral that have attracted authors to it at certain moments in history? How is poetry capable of conveying aspects of experience which prose is not? These are the kinds of questions we intend these courses to ask and, if possible, to answer. In attempting to examine as many facets of a given mode of expression as possible, courses should strive for chronological and geographical range as well. They may be taught in a variety of ways—through lectures or discussions, with the greater emphasis on theory or practice, with or without particular stress on social and historical contexts. But a close examination of literary technique and content should be common to all courses.

This initial formulation of the literature requirement changed very little during subsequent faculty discussions. Some critics thought the insistence on major artists, masterpieces, and mainstream traditions was unduly restrictive; a few argued for further limitations on the ground that some genres are more important than others. But the only significant revision was a statement that "students will be exposed to a variety of critical approaches"—a concession to numerous scholars who feared that ways of describing and explaining literature might be overshadowed by the emphasis on great books.

Course B: Fine Arts or Music The objectives here were analogous to those of the literature courses: to increase students' visual and aural perception, to give them some knowledge of the means of artistic expression, to enable them to judge quality with discrimination, and to acquaint them with a few selected masterpieces. Core planners recommended that each offering deal with a topically defined range of art or music and that "rudimentary lessons" in perception be given, with the greater part of each course left "for dealing directly with the masterpieces themselves."

Some members of the faculty took a dim view of the possibility of advancing students, in a single semester, much beyond the level of rudimentary instruction in fine arts and music. They argued for a full-year course or for a single course above the introductory level that assumed some prior study of the subject. The underlying concern, which appeared in the discussion of other areas as well, was that the Core might become merely a collection of basic skills courses. But those who taught music and fine arts thought the job could be done, or at least should be attempted. This element of the plan went forward without further challenge.

More persuasive were criticisms of the constraints applied to the fine arts area. One irritated professor argued that the definitions proposed for the visual arts were "so narrowly limited to a gentleman's Grand Tour that they miss the esthetic experience of 80 percent of mankind today, most of the arts before the Renaissance, nearly all abstract questions raised by recent scholarship (from psychology and semiotics to

iconology or archaeology) and much of contemporary experimentation." This stinging rebuke led Core planners to loosen
their guidelines somewhat. The strong emphasis on major
works and on questions of visual form and expression remained, but a comparable focus was put on the relationship
between an art and the culture in which it is produced, on
different critical-historical approaches, and on the range of expression revealed in the work of artists active in different times
and places. These additions to the guidelines seemed likely, in
the view of most teachers in the field, to increase the attractive-
ness both of teaching and of enrolling in Core courses.

Another barrage of criticism came from practitioners in
Harvard's relatively new Department of Visual and Environmental Studies because the initial guidelines ruled out practical
exploration of the arts through studio projects. Echoing the
argument of scientists that "one can only learn science by doing
it," practitioners challenged the assumption that only traditional academic disciplines could show students how to comprehend and respond to works of art. This challenge was
accommodated by the understanding that studio courses would
be acceptable in the Core program if they included as a substantial component the study of major works and important
artists.

Course C: Contexts of Culture   This subdivision was originally designed to integrate the students' prior study of literature and the arts—to illustrate appropriate connections among
the arts and to place artistic achievements in their social and
historical contexts. But the Core planners became convinced
that such a sequencing of courses would prove unmanageable.
So they redesigned this subdivision to be an independent com-
plement to the sharply focused literature and arts courses.
Contexts courses were to deal with broad themes, concepts or
movements. They might, for example, focus on a specific time

and place such as Periclean Athens or Medicean Florence, and examine significant literary, artistic, and philosophical works in their particular social context. Alternatively, they might take up a theme in intellectual history that appears in a number of cultures, for example, country versus city or concepts of the happy man. Or courses in this category might look at the works of a particular aesthetic movement such as Neoclassicism or Impressionism. Still others might address the creative process itself, for example, how great artists such as Shakespeare or Beethoven resolved the artistic and philosophical problems with which they wrestled through a lifetime of creativity. Finally, some courses might look at such phenomena as renaissances or revivals in different countries and times, considering their causes, their shared characteristics, and their effects, and linking them with social and political conditions. The underlying purpose in every case would be to broaden students' understanding of the relationship of literature and the arts to their larger social setting.

Core planners did not intend that the materials of study be confined to the Western tradition, but they did argue that this tradition should predominate in the course listings of any given year. They stressed that the Core program was "designed for American students who are being educated at an institution strongly rooted in the Hellenic and Judeo-Christian traditions. One must learn to know himself, and where he comes from, before attempting to learn about others." This position led to a conflict that surfaced repeatedly in later faculty discussions. On one side were those with a strong bias toward the study of Western thought and institutions, those who believed that American students were woefully ignorant of their own heritage. On the other side were a number of critics, not based exclusively in non-Western fields, who feared that this bias would encourage parochialism and ethnocentrism.

The contexts proposal also drew fire from critics who

thought the guidelines were "too fuzzy" and impractical. Where would teachers be found in the humanities who could handle such interdisciplinary courses? And even if some should venture forth, could they offer anything more than a superficial treatment of their subjects? Defenders of the proposal countered that no one could answer these questions without putting the issues to the test of experience.

As the character of the subdivisions in Literature and Arts took shape, doubts were raised about allocating as much as three requirements to the area. Some argued that two requirements primarily devoted to literature (courses A and C) were too much, given other concerns and priorities; others thought that two were an irreducible minimum. The possibility of making contexts courses optional so that students who wished to do so could spend more time on another Core area was raised at a late stage of discussion. No action was taken but such a change was not precluded for the future.

A Note on Expository Writing The Wilson Task Force had declared that "there is no Core requirement to which we attach greater importance than writing: it is fundamental to all other modes of learning." Although the Bailyn formulation did not include expository writing as an integral part of the Core program, the case for keeping it as a "related" college-wide requirement scarcely needed to be made, for there is no conviction more universally held by college teachers than that most students neither enter nor depart from college with the capacity to write acceptable prose.

According to Dr. Richard Marius, who was recruited in 1978 to raise the quality of the college's Expository Writing Program, the problem with Harvard freshmen was not a lack of verbal facility or an inability to construct sound grammatical sentences. But they tended to view certain forms of punctuation—the comma and semicolon in particular—as decorative adornments rather than useful devices in a sentence. And the discipline of spelling apparently struck many students as an intolerable shackling of the human spirit. A more vexing difficulty was the common ignorance of the principles of simple rhetoric: making an argument based on evidence; beginning an argument with a thesis, continuing to a proof, and reaching a relevant conclusion. Freshman papers, Marius reported, very often "start with one thing and end with another, and the road in between is marked by digression, confusion and general clutter."

In an appendix to their report, members of the summer working group in Literature and Arts gave due obeisance to the need for a greater effort to improve the quality of students' expository writing. The specific purposes of instruction were undisputed: students must be trained to write with clarity, precision, and cogency. The question was how to do it. Virtually all parties agreed that a semester course, however well organized, was not sufficient. It had to be supplemented first by additional tutoring for students in the freshman year and beyond, whose capacity to express themselves on paper was substandard. Second, an important opportunity to advance or reinforce a student's writing ability existed in every research paper or essay prepared for a course. Unfortunately, many instructors let these opportunities slip away by adopting the prevalent student view that it was not sporting to uphold standards of grammar and literary expression in anything but writing courses.

Inescapably there was the problem (as hoary as any that beset the academy) of how best to organize the required semester course in expository writing. Core planners claimed that it had become an academic stepchild: the least prestigious form of teaching, characterized by heavy workloads and low pay. Of course there were some dedicated and effective writing teachers, but many writing sections were staffed by instructors trained for (and unable to secure) other kinds of academic work. Even in the "good old days" at Harvard and elsewhere, when members of the English faculty routinely shared in such instruction, it was often viewed not as a challenge but as drudgery. What was new was the size of the discrepancy between professions of the importance of students writing well and the faculty's willingness to commit its time and resources to the attainment of that end.

Those closely acquainted with Harvard's writing program argued that in the last decade or more its courses had drifted from their essential purpose. Marius made the point as charitably as possible:

> I have sat in on some splendid discussions of poetry or of short stories like Faulkner's "A Rose for Emily" or O'Connor's "Everything That Rises Must Converge" or of essays like E.B. White's "Once More to the Lake." I have heard discussions of what it is like to be a woman and what it is like to be a scientist and what it is like to be a member of this ethnic group or that. And I think that most of these excellent discussions—maybe all of them—have been a total waste of time as far as the teaching of writing is concerned.

The problem with such discussions, often used to generate ideas or to "inspire" students, was that "writing is scarcely ever mentioned." Marius argued that "at its best a writing course should be a course in perception and thought." For this purpose courses should focus on the analysis of evidence presented in texts. The best rule of classroom procedure was not to discuss anything until after students had written about it. Core planners agreed. The thrust of their recommendations was that more time and resources must be invested in developing students' capacity to write and that instruction must focus on writing as a craft, not as an extension of the psyche.

Historical Study

The Core planners based their formulation of a history requirement on two principles expressed initially by Professor Bernard Bailyn. First, they argued that an educated person should comprehend history as a form of inquiry and understanding, that is, as a basic mode of studying the human condition. Second, they believed that an educated person should have a sense of the complexity of human affairs, "the way in which a variety of forces—economic, cultural, religious, political—interact with individual aspiration and with the deliberate efforts of individuals to control and shape events." Working from these "core" values—core not in the sense that they constituted the essence of historical study but in that they offered lessons of lasting value to all undergraduates —the planners chose to divide required history courses into two groups, each with a distinctive pedagogical goal.

Group One courses were to deal with the background and development of major, global or near-global issues in the contemporary world. These would seek a historical explanation of such phenomena as the economic inequality of nations, political ideologies, or the role of science in society. Ideally they would show how historical study helps to make sense of the great issues of our time. Some professional historians whom the Core planners consulted thought the conception of these courses was "too presentist." There was, they implied, an unbridgeable gulf between understanding the past in its own terms and showing its relevance to contemporary concerns. But the Core planners saw no conflict. They were prepared to consider courses dealing with discontinuities, past events that have no significant bearing on the present, provided that "they also fulfill the purpose of accounting historically for important intellectual and social issues in the present world."

Group Two courses were to take students away from the

contemporary world and focus their attention on the docu-
mented details of some transforming event in the distant past
—an event that was once a matter of explicit controversy but
that now could sustain objective analysis in historical perspective. Students were to observe, as uninvolved witnesses,
the complexity of events, "the confusion of circumstance,
purpose, and accident that inevitably shapes people's lives," in
short, the process of history. They were to learn that "in
concrete situations of everyday life there are very few heroes
and very few villains, and that only false history makes easy
judgments possible." The content of courses might vary considerably, focusing on such major events as the Protestant
Reformation, the Thirty Years' War, the American Revolution,
or the Darwinian controversy. But all would concentrate on
significant, controversial, and manifest, not latent, events that
irreversibly shaped some portion of the recorded past.

A vocal group of critics, many of them historians, objected
to the "narrow and exclusionary" formulation of Group Two
courses. Why so much emphasis on controversial events? And
even if this was desirable, were there any such events that did
not continue to elicit varied—and controversial—interpretations? Why stress "manifest, not latent" developments,
thereby excluding major historical processes such as the price
revolution of the sixteenth century, the agricultural transformation of the eighteenth century, urbanization in the nineteenth century? Why should the examination of the past be
limited to topics resting on a documentary base and providing
evidence for the analysis of individual motivation? Why leave
out whole realms of historical inquiry such as archaeololgy?

The broad counterargument to these critics was that a looser
definition of aims inevitably would result in nothing more than
a distribution requirement. The present design, for better or
worse, identified two among the many possible goals of a
history requirement and justified them in terms consonant with

the intentions of other Core areas. If the end result smacked of an "authoritarian program," the Core planners rested their case (to paraphrase Finley Peter Dunne on corporation lawyers) on the assertion that what looks like a stone wall to the ordinary man can be a triumphal arch to the imaginative teacher.

Critics outside the history guild also found much to argue with in this formulation. On the whole, they were less concerned about the details of the proposal than with its general thrust. Yet surprisingly, of all the original Core area designs this one changed least through the subsequent debates, perhaps because Bailyn's emphasis on analysis and on students' cognitive development was well suited to the emerging Core program. In a curious way the history proposals acted as a litmus test of the faculty's readiness to depart from a more traditional—a subject- or knowledge-based—conception of general education.

The original Wilson plan had not included history per se as a Core area, assuming that it would be studied under the rubrics of Western Culture and Nonwestern Civilizations and Cultures. Wilson's task force thought that the value of history for the Core lay primarily in providing students with a knowledge of their own past. This would not necessarily breed ethnocentric attitudes, they argued. Indeed, the greater danger was that without courses in this area students would not be able to understand the institutions, ideas, and values of their society. Their case was not simply that students lacked a sense of history or a common fund of historical knowledge (which everyone agreed was so), but that they specifically needed to understand Western history as part of their own intellectual patrimony.

The Wilson formula found many adherents in the faculty. Indeed, when the detailed Core proposal was put to a vote in the spring of 1978, an amendment substituting courses in the history of Western thought for courses on historical process and perspective enjoyed widespread, though insufficient, support. There were, as well, critics of both the Wilson and Bailyn approaches, but they were no more successful. They tended to rally to the standard of a single required survey of Western civilization, the kind of course that would provide a solid chronological framework to remedy the often startling ignorance of students about the sequence of major events and movements in Western history. A statement of the case for such an alternative came from a 1977 Harvard graduate who complained to the *Harvard Crimson* that his own education had been marred by a lack of detailed factual information that would have enabled him to make sense of the welter of theories and interpretations he encountered in his undergraduate studies. He was troubled by the faculty's "obsession with analysis," which meant that students learned only "a bucketful of scholarly interpretations of 'feudalism' or 'development.' "

Supporters of the Bailyn approach appealed to a somewhat different sense of pedagogical reality. One problem with the survey of Western civilization was that it was often boring for both faculty and students. Many students had studied "the facts" of history in high school; while such exposure was by no means universal, it was surely widespread. In any case, the facts of history—without derogating their importance—appear to be infinitely forgettable. Moreover, it seemed highly improbable that faculty members would undertake responsibility for such a course with any degree of continuing enthusiasm. The utility of a Western civilization requirement would also depend entirely on strict sequencing: this course would have to be taken before all the other courses for which it was supposed to provide background. That was likely to interfere with course sequences needed for certain concentrations and with other basic college requirements. But the most compelling argument was that the history component of the Core should be consistent with the program's underlying emphasis on analysis and cognitive development and with the faculty's prevailing historical orientation.

Social Analysis and Moral Reasoning

The Wilson proposal made Modern Social Analysis and Political and Moral Philosophy separate elements of the Core. The aim of Social Analysis was to familiarize students "with at least one important method or perspective for analyzing the workings of modern society or some significant component of it." This brief statement of purpose did little more than reserve a place in the Core for the social science disciplines. Political and Moral Philosophy was more sharply defined. Its explicit goal was "to bring the student to grips with important questions of choice and value by thinking systematically, and in the light of major writings on the subject, about (for example) justice, legitimacy, obligation, or ethical choice in concrete cases." Under pressure to reduce the number of categories, the Faculty Council managed to find a common bond in the systematic analysis of social and ethical problems, and joined the two into an area eventually called Social Analysis and Moral Reasoning.

Social Analysis   The Core planners in social analysis did not see their charge as developing guidelines for introductory social science courses. Such courses belonged in the curricula of the departments. Nor did they believe that it was possible or desirable to define a core of substantive knowledge that all students should possess. Instead they tried to identify those features of social science analysis that seemed most appropriate to a Core requirement and to emphasize the central issues addressed by particular disciplines. The chief task in constructing a Core course, according to the economist Richard Caves, would be to find a line of compromise between the procedural and the substantive importance of the material included. This trade-off, he observed, had not been evident in traditional thinking about general education requirements.

After much debate and consultation with faculty colleagues, the planners came up with a set of principles. All social analysis courses were to address questions of major importance in understanding human behavior and to discuss them in a theoretically coherent manner. How does one rationally allocate scarce resources among competing ends? What theories have been offered to explain war, revolution, crime, human nature, child development, the role of women and of the family, and how does one assess their validity? Courses were to be selected with regard to (1) the significance of the problem to be solved or explained; (2) the application of a major body of theory— and the bigger the theory the better—to the facet of behavior under study; and (3) the presence of a substantial body of empirical data derived from historical experience or from experimental or statistical sources that would permit testing theory and fostering an understanding of the uses and limits of social science data. Thus courses devoted to pure theory, technique, or description of social institutions were ruled out of consideration.

Critics took issue with four aspects of the proposal. Some historically oriented social scientists such as Daniel Bell were troubled by the strong emphasis on analytic techniques, fearing that courses might dwell too much on methodology (always a subject for controversy in the social sciences). Advocates of "old-style" General Education thought the focus on contemporary social concerns and public policy issues in early drafts of the proposal was excessive: shouldn't there be a place here for the history of social thought? Some anthropologists detected a bias against small non-Western cultures in the emphasis on understanding *modern* societies. A broader complaint was that the formulation assumed the existence of generally accepted bodies of fact and undisputed methodologies that need only be mechanically applied. But within the realm of social analysis there were "worlds of discourse hermetically sealed against each other." Shouldn't Core courses seek to break those seals and introduce students to the range of intellectual debate on important issues that cut across—or transcended—particular disciplines, particular methodologies?

In response, the planners argued that the courses they had in mind did not focus on specific methods but more broadly on intellectual *approaches* within which those methods were necessary and useful. The point of an "approach," Michael Walzer explained, is that

> it assumes the existence of something which is to be approached. An approach is like a path: it leads somewhere, not everywhere. It's not like a primary good, which is said to be useful whatever one's interests are . . . The intellectual approaches we prescribe should bring students closer . . . to substantive knowledge of some intellectual issues on which big guns can be brought to bear—major writers, explanatory theories, masses of evidence. Students are to learn something about the guns, something about the "zeroing-in" process, something about the target.

The planners certainly did not intend to rule out courses that would test competing theories. Indeed, such courses were viewed as highly desirable. But neither did they want to exclude courses applying a single mode of analysis, providing that maximum usage was extracted from the particular mode by making its assumptions explicit and examining its major defects. All Core courses in social analysis were to have the common feature of presenting an organized and coherent way of asking and answering important questions about human behavior in modern society. Beyond that, the particular methods, skills, and topics might vary considerably.

Moral Reasoning Addressing an audience of professional school faculty in 1976, Derek Bok asserted that "there has seldom been a period when so many moral problems seem to press upon the society from so many directions." Traditional guides to action—family, faith, and cultural norms—"no longer seem to have the influence they once enjoyed." Whether or not ethical standards have declined as a result, Bok argued, "most people seem to think that they have, and this belief in itself can erode trust and spread suspicion in ways that sap the willingness to behave morally toward others." He thought that universities could make an important contribution to society by developing students' sensitivity to moral questions arising in their own lives and by teaching them that it is both possible and responsible to make carefully reasoned judgments.

Picking up on Bok's concern, the Wilson Task Force outlined a Core area in political and moral philosophy that would lead students to confront important questions of practical choice in politics, law, and ethics. The proposal proved to be compelling, despite a certain reluctance to undertake responsibility for the moral education of students. Between the Wilson formulation and the final Core proposal, several abortive efforts were made to enlarge the scope of this area, to change the title to Philosophical Analysis and include a broader range of subject matter. It was argued that the great traditions and themes of social and philosophical thought, which were worthy of study for their own sake, belonged here and that an understanding of, for example, epistemological issues was no less important for students' intellectual development than learning the intricacies of ethical argument.

But once again faculty sentiment went against a primary focus on the history of ideas. Epistemological issues seemed less urgent or appropriate, and professional philosophers were aghast at the notion that the majority of students could handle or profit from a brief exposure to analysis of complex and technical problems in their discipline.

As the operating plan for a set of courses in moral reasoning evolved, it attempted to meet the needs of three types of students. The first consisted of those who came to college with moral ideals of one sort or another but were unable to articulate their asumptions or defend their conclusions against the sometimes painful attack of their contemporaries. The second group, perhaps the largest, was made up of skeptics who believed that moral positions were essentially a matter of taste and that more or less disguised self-interest was the only rational basis of choice among alternative actions. The third group consisted of students who had learned to make ethical decisions rationally and wished to know what could be said for and against competing theories of utilitarianism, natural law, contract, and consent.

Core courses were to begin by stating one or more major problems of individual or collective choice and value. Is it reasonable or even prudent to be virtuous? What makes the state legitimate? How can war be justified? Is human life sacrosanct? What justification can be found for law and punishment? Students were to be led to alternative answers offered by major philosophers and to learn that all answers are subject to rational criticism. The aim, however, was not to convey the best that has been thought and said in the realm of moral philosophy, but to teach students how to distinguish a good argument from a bad one and, ultimately, how to make reflective judgments about what is right and wrong. In developing courses to satisfy the requirement, this practical objective was of paramount importance. Of course, ethical decisions cannot be made in a factual vacuum, and almost every kind of factual information—historical, sociological, anthropological, psychological, economic, biological, and so on—has some bearing on an important question of choice and value. A course on medical ethics, for example, must include a substantial amount and variety of factual material in order to define the problem to be considered. One could argue that any course providing factual information will help students to think seriously about such issues as justice, obligation, personal responsibility, citizenship, friendship. But for Core courses in moral reasoning the crucial consideration must be the degree to which factual material is used to give students *actual experience* in thinking about ethical problems.

There was no disputing that the emphasis in this subdivision of the Core Program should be on Western thought, institutions, and practices. These Core courses would have to speak to significant moral concerns within the students' own world, for "until they have learned to take their own morality seriously, they can hardly do justice to anyone else's."

Science

The Wilson Task Force offered a relatively simple and straightforward statement of objectives for Core science courses: to acquaint students with science as a way of looking at important parts of the natural world. To this end, courses were to treat in depth one or more topics chosen for their utility in introducing students to important scientific findings and the methods employed to reach them. It was assumed that although courses were to be listed under two distinct headings, Physical Sciences and Biological Sciences, there were no significant differences between them in the mode of scientific reasoning. Thus students might choose two courses from one group or one course from each. A separate requirement was set up in the field of mathematical reasoning and its applications. Wilson's plan included an option permitting well-prepared students to meet Core requirements by examination, and the assumption was that this option would be most often used in science and mathematics.

Responding to criticism from physical scientists who objected to an arrangement that allowed students to avoid quantitative science courses, and from experimental behavioral scientists who felt that their subjects were excluded altogether, the Faculty Council replaced Wilson's fields with an omnibus area called Mathematics and the Behavioral and Natural Sciences. The new grouping implied an emphasis on pure mathematics and on how the natural world may be viewed in its mathematical aspect. But this gesture did not allay the fears of physical scientists, who suspected that belief in a magically simplified "royal road" to learning underlay all conceptions of general education in science.

That suspicion flared in the midst of debate in May 1977, when the Faculty Council announced its intention to introduce students to "the vocabulary of science and its use in the study of natural and human phenomena." Those present at the faculty meeting who had not witnessed earlier faculty reactions (principally in 1959) to President Conant's strong emphasis on the history of science were bewildered by the ferocity of resentment over the use of the word "vocabulary." It seemed somehow to sum up a crucial difference between scientists and laymen, between those who understood the scientific enterprise "from the inside" and those who viewed it from without. Scientists held that the essence of a general introduction to their field was a "mastery of the ideas, methods and principles underlying exemplary scientific areas" rather than "the acquisition of a wide, but superficial vocabulary of science." What they perceived in the Core proposal was another version of the older General Education Program: the hoary, naive, and false assumption of nonscientists that science was based on "the scientific method," with the inevitable consequence, despite disclaimers, of an emphasis on the "soft" historical, philosophical, and sociological approach to science. Stunned by the assault, the Faculty Council humbly retreated. It had used the word "vocabulary" inadvertently; floor critics were invited to communicate with scientists appointed by the dean to formulate the details of a Core requirement in science.

The final Core proposal called for courses that would cover a limited number of important topics in a particular field of science. These topics would be chosen because they cast light on fundamental concepts and principles—what scientists believed to be true. Students were to learn how scientists went about their work—the role of hypothesis, observation, experiment, logical and mathematical calculation—not by discussing "the scientific method" but by studying examples of scientific analysis and experimentation that illustrated basic ideas. Core planners did not rule out historical and social perspectives, and they encouraged interdisciplinary topics, provided that the main emphasis of each course was on key concepts and the way in which they have been developed and validated.

Courses in pure or abstract mathematics were eliminated in favor of a greater emphasis on physical science. Mathematical skills necessary to attack problems in the physical sciences were to be taught in the courses themselves, and some were expected to have a substantial mathematical component. Every science course also was expected to have laboratory sessions or other means—exercises, problem sets—of actively engaging students in the workings of science. Finally, courses were to be divided into two groups, A and B, distinguished by their approach and methodololgy rather than by subject matter. Courses in the A group would deal with physical and chemical systems that were sufficiently well understood to be described in mathematical and quantitative terms. Courses in the B group were to deal with the more complex and less well understood biological and geological systems that could not be fully explained on the basis of the behavior of their simple elements.

Students would be required to choose one course in each group, thereby gaining exposure to the relatively simple, abstract, and analytical as well as the more complex, concrete, and descriptive aspects of scientific inquiry. Cynics suggested that this strategy was merely a device to ensure a place for the "soft" branches of science such as organismic and evolutionary biology. But it could not be denied that under the new formulation no student could avoid contact with the "hard" physical sciences.

The focus on a narrow range of topics within each course was presumed to serve the intellectual interests of instructors as well as the scientific education of students. But under these conditions it seemed improbable that students could be appropriately prepared in high school to "test out" of a science requirement.[1] Moreover, the entire Core program in science was viewed by scientists as an irreducible minimum. Those students with a good high school background—as well as those who wished to pursue their scientific education beyond the minimum rquirement—were to be accommodated in Core courses that presupposed an elementary understanding of certain basic concepts and theories. Or they could substitute suitable courses in the physical and biological or behavioral sciences at a more advanced level. But no student would be exempted from serious study of science at the college level.

It was precisely this bottom line that forged a new and surprising alliance of critics, drawn from the physical sciences, mathematics, and the humanities, against the Core proposal. Some physicists remained unconvinced of the requirement's viability. They believed that "serious" science instruction could flourish only in departments; they favored, at most, a distribution requirement that would leave instruction in departmental hands. An influential segment of the physical scientists considered a mere year of course work insufficient to convey an understanding of the substance and methods of science. A few mathematicians and humanists argued that the proposed burden on students was intolerable. Whether because of innate incapacity or the arduousness of the task of mastering scientific and mathematical concepts, a significant proportion of students would be strained beyond their abilities. One self-confident humanist pronounced himself a "mathematical idiot" and recalled with obvious pain the "scars on my psyche that I can never forget" from a physics course in his Harvard undergraduate days. Mathematics Professor George W. Mackey declared that

> all efforts to bring science to more than a small minority of the educated public are doomed to failure—unless and until some dramatic breakthrough in our understanding of the operation of the nervous system brings about a learning revolution. In the meantime attempts to solve the problem by designing new courses and reorganizing the curriculum seem to me to be as much a waste of time as trying to design a perpetual motion machine before a revolution in physics repeals the law of conservation of energy.

Rosovsky caucused with the planners who had developed working papers for each Core area. None were sympathetic to the view that some significant proportion of Harvard undergraduates were incapable of learning "real" science. But the question of how much time—how many courses—should be allocated to science produced fierce and protracted debate. Standing behind the Wilson Task Force recommendation that Core requirements consume no more than one full year—eight courses—of undergraduate study, Rosovsky dug in his heels against pressure to increase the sum of requirements. If more than two courses were allocated to science, the commitment to other Core areas would have to be reduced. When the smoke cleared from the battlefield, it was plain that although a majority of the whole group of planners wanted students to range more broadly in the field of scientific knowledge, they were not prepared to sacrifice other activities that they viewed as equally important intellectually. The peace proposal made provision for a "Core-related" requirement that would supply to Core science teachers a student population already trained to some minimum standard of competence in quantitative reasoning.

The Quantitative Reasoning Requirement   While the chief spur to develop a degree requirement in quantitative reasoning came from debate on the nature and scope of science instruction, the Wilson Task Force had also made an independent case for the importance of exposing all students to "mathematical reasoning and its applications." So it was neither surprising nor incongruous that quantitative reasoning now joined expository writing and foreign languages—basic skills that were set apart from the Core program proper and treated as "related" issues. Development of standards in these areas proceeded independently under the aegis of separate faculty committees, though very much under the influence of the attitudes and values that were shaping the Core program in general.

The quantitative reasoning committee took a broad view of student needs and curricular interests in working out the details of a requirement. Their proposal tried to meet several objectives. First, it sought to help students acquire the tools to make intelligent assessments of the flood of numerical and statistical data that inundates daily life, and to give them a working knowledge of the basic quantitative concepts needed in almost every field of college study. A second aim was to introduce students to the use of computers and to the capabilities and limitations of this adaptable new intellectual tool.

An emphasis on applications was deemed essential. The planning group, chaired by Professor of Mathematics Andrew Gleason (who had been an early advocate of the "new math" in primary and secondary school curricula), believed that this was the weakest aspect of students' prior training in mathematics as well as the one most widely called upon in college studies. Gleason noted that although the mean score of Harvard freshmen on the S.A.T. math test was over 700— and almost all of the freshmen scored above the national average for high school students—too many students were unable to use what they had learned. It was also true that between a third and a half of entering freshmen failed to qualify for placement in the college's first-year mathematics course. Some who arrived with advanced placement credentials even failed sections of the qualifying exam dealing with pre-calculus materials.

But Gleason wished to avoid at all costs a formulation of the requirement that could be linked to the sequence of mathematics instruction in secondary schools. His committee believed that it would be a grave pedagogical mistake to try to go over the material that students had failed to master in high school. The relatively low success rate of remedial math courses convinced them that students should be given a fresh start by replacing the formalistic approach of high school mathematics with a self-evidently relevant applied or quantitative reasoning approach. Gleason also feared that if the standard was set at, say, introductory calculus, then students who had not had the opportunity to study, or encountered difficulty, at that level might be discouraged from applying to Harvard. Yet if the standard was set at a lower level, it could well discourage students from pursuing more advanced work in secondary schools. In any case, it made more sense to zero in on the notorious discrepancy between students' theoretical knowledge and their ability to apply it in other contexts.

The proposed requirement consisted of three parts: (1) applications of the function concept, with emphasis on linear functions and methods of extrapolation and interpolation; (2) uncertainty and statistical reasoning, with emphasis on the intuitive nature of probability distributions, how to fit straight lines to empirical data, the advantages and pitfalls of different sampling methods, and the kinds of questions to ask when assessing the validity of statements made on the basis of statistical information; and (3) computer use, enabling students to learn basic aspects of programming and how to use Harvard's computer facilities. The computing portion of the requirement represented a significant innovation at Harvard, inspired in part by the successful program at Dartmouth College and sharing with it the conviction that an ignorance of computers will become a handicap to students in the future. But this part of the requirement was also integral to the larger conception stressing the broad and practical applications of mathematics, and to that aspect of the Core Curriculum which sought to demonstrate the uses of knowledge.

Planners hoped that a great majority of students would be able to prepare through self-study for examinations covering parts one and two of the requirement. To assist them, a sizable group of undergraduates, former students, and faculty members later set to work developing study guides, workbooks, and practice tests. (A one-semester elective course covering the same material was also designed.) For the third part of the requirement they devised self-study guides designed to familiarize students with the Harvard computer system and simple programming languages, as well as a two-week minicourse for students who had no prior experience using computers. Thus the strategy relied heavily on guided self-help rather than formal instruction. Taken together with the emphasis on applications to real life situations, it was a strategy well suited to the diverse preparation of students. It might even have some appeal to those students suffering from "math anxiety."

Foreign Cultures

The Wilson Task Force expected the areas of both Western Culture and Nonwestern Civilizations and Cultures to contribute to the general humanistic education of Harvard students. But the primary purpose of the non-Western cultures provision was to expand their range of cultural experience. The theory was that learning about social systems significantly different from their own would increase their cosmopolitanism, a quality deemed essential in the modern world.

But when the Faculty Council revamped Wilson's categories with an eye to greater and more consistent emphasis on disciplined approaches to knowledge, a separate set of non-Western studies seemed anomalous. Some argued that these materials were best treated in the Core areas of Literature and Arts, Historical Study, and Social Analysis. But there was a countervailing concern that, freighted with other objectives, most Core courses would be unable to convey a sufficiently rich appreciation of "foreign" cultural systems. Moreover, complaints were raised that Wilson's broad differentiation of Western and non-Western civilizations did not sufficiently distinguish among language cultures.

The Core planners set out to reconstruct an area of foreign culture studies based on the major civilizations of Europe, Asia, Africa, and South America. Courses were to use literary, visual, historical, and social science materials and modes of analysis, but also, whenever possible, they were to emphasize language as a means of entry into another culture. They were not only to introduce other cultures per se but, ideally, to give attention to issues in the past or present that would permit students to gain a greater perspective on American society. For these purposes it seemed important to probe deeply into selected aspects, problems, or distinctive features of a culture rather than offer comprehensive coverage. If it turned out that courses in other Core areas also met these aims, so much the better: students could meet two requirements with a single course.

Core planners argued that the foreign cultures studied should be living ones and should represent major cultural traditions outside the English-speaking nations. These were divided into two groups, and the principle was adopted that the less foreign a culture, the more advanced should be its study. The first group of courses, embracing the major societies of Western Europe and Latin America, would either be conducted entirely in the relevant language or students would be expected to read largely original-language texts. In the second group, major cultures of the non-Western world, in view of the language barrier texts would be read in translation.

The first objection to this formulation came from classicists, who found themselves excluded by the emphasis on "living cultures." Did anyone seriously contend that study of the ancient civilizations of Greece and Rome inherently failed to meet the Core's objectives? No one did, so the prescription was altered to read "primarily, but not exclusively, living cultures." Next came a series of criticisms from anthropologists who decried the bias toward major civilizations, thus echoing the protest from other quarters that the entire Core program, with its repeated emphasis on masterpieces and major artists, authors, and thinkers, suffered from "the provincialism of greatness." What was more, the abandonment of a category devoted exclusively to the study of non-Western cultures reinforced the suspicion that Core planners meant to assert the primacy of Western civilization. At the extreme, one faculty member maintained that the very conception of a foreign culture category that stressed differences rather than similarities was profoundly ethnocentric. It divided humanity into "us" and "them," thereby failing to recognize that "there is only one civilization and one culture, that of man." These objections were overruled largely on the practical grounds that one had to draw a line somewhere and that the critics had offered no better proposal than the one recommended by Core planners.

The Foreign Language Requirement   Ever since the ill-fated move of the Wilson Task Force to strike down what it viewed as a pro forma language requirement, Core planners, with Rosovsky in the lead, had insisted that the question of a degree requirement in a foreign language be distinguished from the foreign culture aspect of the Core program. Although the Core was designed to encourage students who already possessed language skills to maintain and advance them, inevitably it affected thinking about the level of proficiency necessary for a meaningful language requirement, the problem of those who had special disabilities in learning languages, and the appropriate balance between speaking and reading skills. As it unfolded, the Core emphasized the ability to read a foreign language, although this went against the grain of more than a decade of concern with speaking skills in language instruction. Behind the scenes there was a great deal of murmuring to the effect that the language learning disability ("strephosymbolia") afflicting roughly 6 percent of undergraduates was the product of aural-oral modes of instruction. "In the old days," one student adviser reported, "we used to tell the kids who couldn't hack French or Spanish to switch to Latin, and they managed pretty well."

To move somewhat ahead of the story, the separate faculty committee appointed by Rosovsky in 1979 proved unable to resolve the thorny issues involved in reformulating the foreign language requirement. It produced a vigorous plea for a strengthened requirement, couched in terms of the intrinsic value and general utility of language study. Committee members agreed that the existing standard, a C.E.E.B. score of 560, was inadequate. And the "residency option," which permitted students to satisfy the requirement with two semesters of coursework even if they did not achieve a 560 proficiency level, came in for sharp criticism. But raising the proficiency standard to a C.E.E.B. score of 600 would run into a series of painful consequences. First, a higher standard and elimination of the residency option would affect the choice of languages to be studied. Students would shy away from Slavic languages, Chinese, or Japanese, because it would be much harder to meet the standard in the more difficult languages. Second, estimates indicated that without a residency "cap" a significant propor- tion of students would need three, four, five, or more semesters of college study to meet the standard. Greatly influenced by the spirit of restraint and practical compromise that animated Core discussions, supporters of a strengthened requirement recog- nized its potential effect on the total number of undergraduate course requirements and drew back to reconsider whether the "academically praiseworthy" proficiency-only formula ought to be modified by a "sound" residency option. Once again, the issue was left unresolved, pending further clarification of the impact of Core requirements on student programs.

Shaping the Program

Through the fall term of 1977 the central committee, under Rosovsky's insistent chairmanship, took charge of the emerg- ing Core program. In addition to the authors of the area working papers, the committee included President Bok, James Q. Wilson, and several academic and administrative officers who were close associates of Rosovsky—Professors Glen W. Bowersock (classics and history), Edward L. Keenan (history), and Paul C. Martin (physics and applied Sciences), and Deans Phyllis Keller, Charles P. Whitlock, and Edward T. Wilcox. Their job was to work out priorities and negotiate details for each Core area and to present to the faculty a comprehensive plan showing the relationship of the parts to the whole—and of the whole to the overall education of Harvard undergraduates.

The first problem for the central committee was to evaluate

the recommendations in the first-round working papers, which underwent innumerable adjustments and refinements as committee members debated the issues and sought advice from faculty in the areas under study. More than eighty faculty members were involved in these consultations. Simultaneously, the central committee came to grips with structural and procedural problems that inevitably shaped their thinking about substantive issues.

The pairs of faculty members who had worked on area proposals over the summer had not been given explicit limits on the nature or number of course requirements. Yet the work of the various pairs showed a remarkable consistency in pedagogical emphasis, reflecting an underlying consensus on the approach the Core program should take. It was not surprising that the number of areas they proposed corresponded to the number of groups appointed—five. But each group tended to make generous estimates of the number of courses that should be required in its own area.

It soon became clear that the Core's relation to other components of undergraduate education had to be taken into account before judgments could be made as to the relative weight of each area within the program. The central committee's decision to limit the sum of Core demands to no more than one year of undergraduate study, the equivalent of eight courses, was a difficult one, but it set the boundary within which the group had to balance the claims of its members. Assuming that students could qualify for two exemptions by virtue of their work in concentrations, the aims of the five areas would have to be contained within a total of ten courses. This numerical constraint powerfully shaped priorities and strategies within, as well as between, Core areas. The final version of the program assigned three courses to Literature and Arts, two to Historical Study, two to Social Analysis and Moral Reasoning, two to Science, and one to Foreign Cultures:

an allocation reflecting the political and intellectual influence of humanists on the committee and in the faculty.

Once the central committee agreed on boundaries and objectives, it faced two further tasks: including in the guidelines for each area criteria to help future committees decide whether or not to accept a course for inclusion in the Core program, and developing a convincing rationale for the program, showing how it fit together and what it intended to accomplish.

Drafting area guidelines was a ticklish problem. It was one thing to agree on educational goals; it was difficult, but not unduly so, to reach a consensus and find the right language to express it. But it was quite another thing to rule on how courses should be organized and taught. No one could predict what policy would prove most effective. Yet without principles of inclusion and exclusion to guide it, a future committee would have no way to ensure the comparability of the courses it sponsored. And unless courses were comparable, the objective of providing students with both a choice and a common intellectual experience would fall by the way.

Gradually, haltingly, the central committee probed its own intentions. Each working paper had stressed that courses should be organized to convey something of fundamental value that transcended its specific subject matter. As a general principle, broad survey courses were ruled out in favor of courses dealing with topics or problems that illustrated a particular mode of analysis and engaged students in its application. In the area of Foreign Cultures, to take the most difficult case, there might be several ways to increase student cosmopolitanism, but the Core guidelines emphasized exploration of cultural differences rather than similarities, to provoke students' reflection on their own society.

The idea that ways of thinking could be taught through varied subject matter had the obvious advantage of reflecting the diverse and changing interests of students and faculty. But courses presenting wholly idiosyncratic approaches to knowledge (Professor X's theory of truth—with perhaps a half-truth in each semester?) also were ruled out; in principle it should be possible for any Core course to be taught by more than one member of the faculty.

The practical decisions written into the Core guidelines underlined the stylistic gulf between the new program and its General Education predecessor. In place of lofty rhetoric and ambitious aims there were complex strictures and limited, sharply defined purposes. Emphasis on a variety of perspectives reflected the widespread faculty assumption that it no longer was possible, if indeed it had ever been, to master a broad range of substantive knowledge in the brief span of four college years. The Core's planners believed that it was more realistic to try to convey to students "the kinds of knowledge that exist in certain important areas, how such knowledge is acquired, how it is used, and what it might mean to them personally." To be sure, the materials of study were to include major works of art, significant and recurrent issues, key theories, concepts, texts, and findings, but these materials were to serve only as starting points. If the Core plan worked, it would provide students of diverse talents, abilities, and prior preparation with the tools and perspectives to advance their own learning. It was modest and future-oriented in the sense that it sought only to foster some significant progress by each student in a number of intellectual directions.

In their final report to the faculty, the architects of the Core explained how their proposals might contribute to the development of the "educated person," which Rosovsky had set forth as the "minimum standard" for Harvard undergraduates. A Core-related requirement provided for training in expository writing to help students think and write clearly, and adjunct requirements in quantitative reasoning and foreign languages rounded out the basic skills. The Core program itself was de-

signed to provide "critical appreciation and informed acquaintance with the ways in which we gain and apply knowledge
and understanding of the universe, of society, and of ourselves." Courses in several areas introduced students to "other
cultures and other times" to establish a wide context for understanding individual experience. Courses in literature, art,
history, and social analysis, reinforcing those in moral reasoning, offered opportunities for students to gain experience in
thinking about moral and ethical problems.

The Core design assumed that concentration and
nonconcentration requirements had different functions in
undergraduate education. Concentration hinges on cumula-
tion or progression—a sequence of study that builds on earlier
accomplishment toward a higher level of proficiency and intellectual autonomy. The Core complemented concentrations
in two ways: by exposing students to alternative ways of
examining and understanding experience, and by providing a
common set of studies for students in different concentrations.
Electives play a variety of roles in undergraduate studies: they
allow some students to pursue their major interest in greater
depth than would ordinarily be the case, others to be dilet-
tantes in the best sense of the word, and still others to develop a
minor concentration in a field of secondary interest. It was
thought that the Core program would enable students to
choose their electives in a more informed way and that their
choices would build on learning acquired through Core studies.
Thus, in theory at least, the main components of the undergraduate curriculum—Core, concentration, and electives—
would have more than a casual relationship to each other.

By late January 1978 the central committee had completed its
consultations and internal deliberations. Within a matter of
weeks the revised text of a thirty-five-page report was delivered
to all members of the faculty. In a covering letter Rosovsky
declared that although the report still was subject to Faculty

Council review, he thought it desirable to distribute it to the full faculty at the earliest possible time. It would be docketed for general discussion at regular faculty meetings in mid-March and again in mid-April. Meanwhile the Council would prepare a separate set of legislative proposals "calling for authorization *to develop* the Core Program and the Core requirements in keeping with the objectives, constraints and strictures articulated in the report." Rosovsky requested that the document be read as a set of guidelines whose "main purpose is to outline goals and norms, and to specify criteria by which course proposals may be evaluated." He expected that the program would have to be developed over a four-year period. There would be an opportunity for further and final review after it became fully operative in September 1982.

The Council's task was to study the guidelines, negotiate with Core planners such changes as seemed desirable, draft enabling legislation, and manage debate on the floor of the faculty. As a general strategy, it was agreed that the Council would first take account of the views of elected student representatives and then work out a procedure for the orderly consideration of faculty reaction.

Student government at Harvard then was organized in part through subcommittees of the Faculty Council. The body concerned with educational affairs was the Committee on Undergraduate Education, composed of equal numbers of Council members and elected students and chaired at that time by Professor of Classics and History Glen Bowersock. That committee in turn worked with an advisory body, called the Educational Resources Group (ERG), composed entirely of student representatives elected from each residential house.

ERG had already gone on record in support of the broad thrust of the Wilson report. It quarreled with some details of content and administrative structure but asserted that it was more concerned with the creation and maintenance of good courses than with the nature of the requirements. That view persisted through its evaluation of the new report. ERG now endorsed the concept of the Core program, and with one or two minor exceptions—most notably a suggestion that the Third World be specifically included among non-Western cultures—offered no critique of the area formulations. However, ERG wanted official student representatives on all Core subcommittees, a pass/fail option for some fraction of Core courses, a choice between the first group of history courses and additional work in some other area, and most importantly, a "limited bypass" option.

The bypass proposal was that students be permitted to substitute two appropriate advanced departmental courses for any single Core requirement. ERG's reason was not that it objected to these requirements; on the contrary, it opposed the suggestion that some students be exempted from the mandatory course in expository writing. In part its argument was that a bypass option would reduce the size of Core courses by providing an alternate route to meeting requirements. But the more crucial consideration was student speculation that not enough advanced courses would be offered within the Core to siphon off those with superior preparation, especially in science. Showing their usual adeptness at making practical calculations, students worried about unfair competition in Core courses.

Council members agreed with ERG that student representatives should attend meetings of the Core subcommittees (except for those dealing with confidential personnel matters), but without voting privileges. They were sympathetic to a no exemption policy for writing courses, but considered it and the pass/fail option matters to be determined by future subcommittees. However, they flatly rejected the limited bypass proposal, believing that such a move would undercut the program before it received a fair trial and turn it into a mere distribution requirement.

Associate Professor of Physics William Skocpol, the one Council member who argued vigorously for the limited bypass (and cast the only negative ballot in a preliminary vote on the Core program), claimed that its inclusion would increase the long-range viability of the program. His reasons were that "the more restricted the set of available offerings, the more necessary it will be for most or all of the courses to be adapted to meet the needs of the students with the least background or interest." In addition, he argued, there were some outstanding full-year courses that seemed to meet Core objectives but were not adaptable to the one-semester format of the program. The Council held its ground: in due time, if it proved desirable and feasible to designate certain pairs of departmental courses as meeting Core purposes, the Core committees could always do so. Eventually, when this issue resurfaced—with explosive force—in the next phase of general faculty discussion, the Council was forced to moderate its stand.

Meanwhile the Council wrestled with a set of legislative proposals designed to usher in the program and set up the necessary committees with appropriate powers. A key issue engendering extensive debate was the scope of the program. How many courses would be offered when it was fully developed? A minority of Council members opposed setting limits in advance; inevitably these would look arbitrary and rigid. A majority argued that the faculty needed to have some idea of what was intended and that a "reasonable" limit would aid subcommittees both in choosing among course prospects and in maintaining the guidelines. It was agreed that the number of offerings might vary from one area to another, but that after full implementation the program "ordinarily" should list no less than eighty and no more than one hundred offerings in any given year. While the discussion proceeded, rumors flew around the campus. A student newspaper announced that the magic number was thirty; ERG went on record as demanding fifty. Faculty members who had remained aloof or neutral toward the reforms became curious about the growing tumult.

Hard Core versus Soft Core: Images of the University College

Distribution of the Core guidelines in February 1978 rekindled widespread faculty interest in the enterprise. Between the March and April faculty meetings, the Core dominated campus conversations. In his introductory remarks at the March meeting, Rosovsky noted that the room had not been so crowded since the late (and unlamented) sixties. To ensure a full hearing of views, Faculty Council strategists had decided that no vote would be taken at the March meeting and no formal amendments or alternative proposals entertained. It had prepared only a preliminary draft of the Core legislation, which it intended to revise in the light of the faculty's reactions. The first meeting was to be a free-for-all discussion.

Rosovsky characterized the Core recommendations as "a modest proposal." It was a statement of educational priorities in the form of requirements. The faculty had already committed itself to the principle of nonconcentration requirements; now the question was whether it was possible to build a consensus on the specifics out of myriad, and sometimes conflicting, opinions and preferences. He thought the proposal in hand was a considerable improvement over the status quo, but it was not cast in concrete. Since no one could know in advance how it might work out, the preliminary legislation simply requested authorization to begin an experiment, to set up a series of faculty committees that would implement the plan gradually over a four-year period, making adjustments, interpretations, and modifications in the light of experience. There were to be seven subcommittees, one for each Core area plus quantitative reasoning and expository writing, and a Standing Committee composed of the seven subcommittee chairmen. Provision was made for a final review in 1983, when the program was fully operational and the faculty could see how the idea translated into practice.

From the chair, President Bok began to work his way down a list of speakers who had requested time to state their opposition, criticism, fears, or anxieties about the program. The speakers fell, more or less, into three broad groups: those who believed the entire approach of the Core was wrong-headed, those who thought the plan possibly was logical but certainly was impractical, and those who were unhappy with some particular element.

The key arguments of the first group reiterated much of what had been said in the debate over Wilson's Task Force report. But now dissent was more sharply focused and explicit. The two main grounds of opposition were that the Core, like its General Education predecessor, misconstrued what it means to be an educated person, and that it falsely asserted the existence of a set of intellectual experiences "each of which independently would be judged by a majority of the Faculty to be important" for an educated person.

According to Professor of Applied Mathematics William Bossert, the Core is "a simple relabeling of what we are already doing badly—namely, generating nondepartmental courses lacking the rigor of departmental offerings, and using them to remedy a perceived lack of breadth in student programs." Bossert thought the Core report defined education in a negative way by saying that "one is not educated if one avoids certain experiences, or lacks facility in certain techniques or is ignorant of certain facts." Candidly confessing his own ignorance of techniques outside his own discipline, he suggested that he was scarcely alone in this regard. He believed that "the summed ignorance of this particular Faculty is a proper demonstration that ignorance in itself is debilitating neither professionally nor personally." The point was an important one, for Bossert articulated fundamental opposition to the pursuit of "extreme—and necessarily superficial—breadth" in undergraduate education. He thought that the distinguishing feature of an educated person is "personal maturity" or the ability to assess one's own situation "with regard to the world and society." He did not believe that Core courses, or elementary courses of any kind, could promote critical analysis at a level that would be personally maturing. For this reason he favored a program of majors and minors that would lead students into advanced work and set them to master at least two subjects at a level productive of genuine understanding and intellectual autonomy.

Sociologist Harrison White was in full agreement. He thought that current students were much abler than their counterparts in 1953 and more accustomed to making decisions for themselves. They did not need to be "herded" into prescribed lecture courses "scattered across the intellectual landscape." Existing departments already enclosed the legitimate subareas of knowledge; they had experience in judging courses and developing curricula. In his view the Core proposal was "extremely mediocre" in its content; it was modern only in the sense that it added a "bureaucratic heft" to older versions of general education. White predicted that the "new committee seats" created by the Core program would drain vitality from teaching, from the development of new courses, and from faculty research.

Without necessarily supporting Bossert's alternatives, other critics attacked the proposition that there was a core of essential knowledge, skills, and habits of thought. Laying out the opposition's case, Mechanical Engineering Professor Frederick

Abernathy pointed to the apparent instability of the Core recommendations from the time of the Wilson report to the present. First there had been eight areas of study, then five, and now ten.[2] "This year language requirements are in, natural sciences are down, literature and the arts are up, foreign languages and cultures are in. How can it be that what is essential has changed so much in the course of a year?" In Abernathy's view, the present proposal represented "a political compromise" designed to attract a sufficient number of faculty votes. But even if it proved acceptable to the faculty, "it is not likely in every case to satisfy the needs and goals of undergraduates." He believed that students came to Harvard to study with a faculty "distinguished for its research and teaching in forty-seven departments or fields of concentration, and to partake of its rich offering of some two thousand courses." Each student had unique aspirations and interests. If it made sense for the faculty to allow students freely "to select their majors and to enter their major fields at the level appropriate to their particular background and ability," then why did it not also make sense to allow students "to elect how they will satisfy a distribution requirement to achieve comparable ends?"

Deferring to the judgment of colleagues who supported the Core proposals, Abernathy and others felt that perhaps the Core should be made the recommended but not the only way of fulfilling a distribution requirement. He was not at all convinced by the counterargument that Harvard graduates should have a shared intellectual experience. Moreover, he believed that the faculty sooner or later would have to back away from applying the full set of Core requirements to students, such as junior transfers, who spent less than four years at Harvard. If adjustments were made for those students, it followed that the principle of a common learning for all Harvard graduates was not sacrosanct.

The other practical consideration raised repeatedly in the

course of discussion was whether the heavy—some called it "Byzantine"—set of Core requirements would discourage the brightest and best-trained high school students from applying to Harvard. That concern also troubled some faculty members, who privately conveyed to Rosovsky a set of objections that were far more practical than philosophical. As summarized by Paul Martin, their belief was that while some courses and ideas were more fundamental and universally applicable than others, there was no sharp, clear-cut division. They didn't see how the faculty could present essential material in a form that was educationally profitable for the majority of students year after year; there was too wide a divergence in the students' backgrounds, abilities, and interests. And there was also the problem of teaching to a captive audience. Even if the faculty "could fix upon a gospel, could we provide the committed and dedicated staff that would spread it year after year in a flexible and educationally valuable fashion?" Where would the funds come from and how would the Core program affect departmental budgets? Unwilling as yet to prejudge the matter, a number of faculty members who were attracted by the idea of specific nonconcentration requirements (as against an ill-defined distribution requirement) believed that the program was still inadequately described. It remained unclear exactly what was required, how it could be achieved, and at what cost.

Some critics of the Core thought its greatest weakness was that it did not go far enough in a desirable direction or take exactly the right road. Professor of Chemistry Frank Westheimer was particularly distraught over the balance—or imbalance—among Core components. He thought there was much in the new curriculum to "supplement the specialization" of science concentrators, and to begin their education in the humanities and social sciences. But students engaged in other concentrations would be misled if they believed that the science requirement was a sufficient minimum. There was no doubt in Westheimer's mind that the Core proposal relegated science to "a minor, perhaps only a trivial, place in the intellectual heritage of mankind." He flatly asserted that it was impossible to provide students with a basis for understanding the role of science in society or to lay the groundwork for future scientific learning through one course devoted to the physical sciences and one to the biological or behavioral sciences. What this meant, in effect, was that students could earn a Harvard B.A. degree by devoting 6 percent of their studies (two out of a total of thirty-two courses) to education in science.

Responding first to the view that there is no generally accepted set of intellectual experiences that every educated person should acquire, Core supporters led off with a statement by Biology Professor E. O. Wilson, who asserted his own "belief in the essential coherence of knowledge." He thought that neither the knowledge explosion nor the specialization of the faculty nor the modest year of study allocated to the program prevented the transmission of a core of knowledge and ways of thinking. In his opinion, the central ideas of intellectual life were "continuously reforming in a way so as to increase in number much less rapidly" than knowledge itself; in some areas they might even be decreasing. He noted, for example,

> that if one knew elementary physics and organic chemistry, one was prepared to enter immediately into the vast and magic world of molecular biology, and to grasp its central ideas in a relatively short period of time; whereas thirty years ago, when the subject was only a minute fraction of what it is today, one had to work just as hard to learn a plethora of terms, fragmentary ideas, and experiments that often seemed like alchemy in their specialized application. So too with evolutionary biology. Today, as a result of real advances in fundamental population biology, it was possible to master the core of evolutionary biology when one learned about ten ideas.

Wilson sensed "a similar implosion in the social sciences." He called for a "deliberate affirmation in universities of the convergence and centrality of a large part of knowledge, of methodololgy, and of the very techniques of reasoning." The Core program would encourage the faculty to look for this common ground and transmit it to students.

Expanding on Wilson's intellectual justification of a Core Curriculum, Michael Walzer began by addressing Bossert's major-and-minor-subject (or distribution) alternative. Bossert had described the effect of his proposal quite accurately, he thought. It would help students reach for "personal maturity" —with emphasis on the adjective. But Walzer believed that for most students this would entail "an area of professional training and an area of personal interest—a profession and a hobby," falling short of what he believed should be expected of students. It was his conviction that the faculty "ought to require students to participate in the general intellectual culture of their society, and to prepare themselves to share intelligently in the collective choices of a democratic state." Personal maturity was something students would achieve personally, but they needed some guidance from the faculty as to "the character of the culture, and the nature and complexity of moral and political choice," none of which are spontaneous discoveries. To shape and frame these discoveries for students, the faculty had to make choices of their own, and *that* was the reason for the elaborate committee structure upon which the Core program rested. Committee members would be required to engage in serious and continuous reflection on the character of the intellectual, social, and political world, to argue with one another, and to find ways to agree. Certainly it would take time and energy, but it was, after all, what the faculty was there for.

Turning to the charge that the Core proposals represented "a political compromise," Walzer noted that the issues before the faculty obviously were matters of deep dispute, "matters about which all members of the Faculty have very deep feelings, even if those feelings are expressed only every twenty years or so." For this very reason, those who worked on the Core proposals "had been unavoidably involved in a kind of curricular politics, a process of mutual accommodation, an effort to reach consensus." They had made concessions "on issues where there were deep intellectual commitments." Westheimer's argument for more science, for example, had "been heard before, and it is a good argument—perhaps too good . . . for it is perfectly clear from what he said that one more course in the sciences would not be nearly enough." Many other faculty members felt that the Core requirements already were too numerous and should be reduced so that the area of free choice might be enlarged. Core planners had been obliged "to balance those demands that were felt from fields whose importance all would recognize, against the equally important and pressing demands of students to maintain some area of election."

Historian Bernard Bailyn found the Bossert proposal "a very appealing one in some ways," but he reminded the faculty that in the early 1960s it had made changes in the original General Education Program to allow students the option of developing a minor field. Just a year ago the faculty had decided that that approach was much too limiting. Bailyn thought the "whole idea" of the Core "was to get away from the practice of doing many more things in more technical ways." In any case, it was very far from a relabeling of the old General Education Program. Where the original program had attempted a broad, surveylike introduction to all of the major areas of knowledge, the Core isolated certain ways of tackling problems in different areas and required students to learn these, not in some abstract way but by actually wrestling with and working through selected sets of problems. There might be a dozen other ways to organize a history requirement, for example, but the Core planners had worked with the idea that history is a major technique employed by at least half the departments in the university. To teach history as technique, Core planners outlined two sets of courses, one set providing historical orientation to major problems of contemporary life and the other reaching into the distant past for a deep perspective on some important and controversial issue that revealed the complex process of human affairs. This was surely not the sort of course envisioned in the Redbook, but it now seemed a useful and attractive way to teach and to learn history, one that would offer students both substantive knowledge and the analytic training necessary to extend it.

Prodded by anxious speculation as to the adverse impact of the Core proposal on undergraduate recruitment, President Bok invited comment from the widely respected dean of admissions, Fred Jewett. Jewett said he could only guess about its probably effect, but over the last two years many prospective students had questioned him about the new curriculum. By and large, their interest was positive. He believed that the very best students were more concerned with the quality of courses and undergraduate teaching than with the character and number of requirements. It was his feeling that these students were greatly impressed with the serious attention paid to educational reform in the course of the faculty's discussions. In any case, most students who elected Harvard expected to have much more structure in their programs than they actually found. What they really wanted was good courses, and any program providing that would meet with general acceptance. To be sure, there was no program that would satisfy every Harvard student; there would always be some opposition to any particular plan. But Jewett could introduce one fact into the discussion: with all of the internal and external publicity given to the Core Curriculum during the year, applications had increased substantially and had reached a historic high point.

This reassurance scarcely quieted the fears of determined Core opponents, for their concern ultimately rested on a set of beliefs about students, education, the character of the university, and its role in society. Physicist Robert Pound summed it up: in contrast to the narrow and "regimented" curriculum under discussion, a rich and unconstrained cirriculum encouraged each student to reach for the highest possible level of achievement. He did not accept the view that if left to their own devices students would "turn away from intellectual concerns" or that college was the last opportunity they would have in life to develop broad interests. A university dedicated to the advancement of scholarship and learning should seek to convey that spirit to students. It had no higher educational mission, "nor ought it to try to substitute for traditional family influences." Ranged against Pound's view were those who believed that specialization was not the exclusive or even the primary aim of undergraduate education, that "education is not a market mechanism," that the Core did not entail a regimented curriculum but offered latitude for student choice within reasonable constraints designed to meet real intellectual needs. They argued that Core courses must appeal to the exceptional student or they would appeal to no one, including instructors. There was always the risk that the program would not live up to expectations, but surely it was worth the effort to try to broaden the intellectual range of students.

The March discussion consumed two highly charged hours; fifteen speakers trooped to and from the microphone. Readings of the outcome varied. Rosovsky thought that everything had been said before. He was torn between the desire to press forward to a vote and apprehension about appearing to stifle debate. He noted with satisfaction that divisions of opinion about the Core did not correspond to the old political cleavages in the faculty, that for the most part they cut across age groups and departmental lines. Core supporters were relatively

optimistic, especially when the results of a faculty poll conducted by the student newspaper showed that about two-thirds
of the respondents intended to vote in favor of the proposal
either in its present form or with "minor revisions." Adding
spice to the stew, *Crimson* headline writers claimed that the
faculty was evenly split by counting those with minor objections as nay-sayers. In the four weeks preceding the April
faculty meeting, behind-the-scenes activity flourished. Formal
amendments, rumors of formal amendments, and just plain
rumors flowed into the Faculty Council. It was said that one
professor intended to call for a secret ballot, implying that peer
pressure mounted by Core advocates had reached a coercive
level. As it turned out, what was intended was a call for a mail
ballot, which was declared improper by the elected parlia-
mentarian because the faculty's rules of procedure restrict such
ballots to constitutional issues.

Sixteen amendments and one alternative plan actually were
proposed to the Faculty Council. Working at a hectic pace, the
faculty's legislative master craftsman, Assistant Dean Edward
T. Wilcox, consulted with each proponent to clarify the
similarities and differences among the amendments and to test
the prospect of combining those that sought comparable goals.
The amendments fell roughly into four categories: (1) those
creating opportunities for students to bypass Core offerings,
(2) those intended to alter the structure or (3) change the
content of the program, and (4) those applying to administrative details. The Faculty Council resolved virtually all administrative issues through minor adjustments in its legislative
proposals.

Most of the amendments fell into the first two categories,
leading Council members to conclude that the Popular Front
issue for critics was the degree of flexibility allowed by the
Core legislation. To be sure, there remained a number of critics
who had made up their minds about the proposal and would

not support it under any circumstance. They believed that Core advocates would not listen to a rational argument against any element of the proposal. But there seemed to be a sizable and possibly decisive number who for various reasons wished to bring the issue of flexibility out in the open. Some thought the proposal would pass in any case and that a major effort to loosen it was therefore essential. Still others believed that administrative flexibility was implicit and could easily be made explicit. A few worried that even with the best of intentions the Core would so strain faculty resources that it could not be effectively implemented, and they wanted to build in provision for future alterations.

Professor Paul Martin, a physicist who as dean of the Division of Applied Sciences worked closely with Rosovsky, took the lead in negotiating two consolidated amendments that presented the interests of the "soft" Core proponents in a form deemed friendly by the Faculty Council. The maneuver typified Martin's role in the entire Core planning process. He did not favor the Core proposal, preferring a distribution requirement based on departmental course offerings. But his interest in undergraduate education (sharpened by his chairmanship of the Task Force on Concentrations), his close relationship to Rosovsky, and his personal reservations about the direction of reform, drew him into the circle of reformers. Throughout the protracted discussions of the Core, Martin played the role of devil's advocate in Rosovsky's inner councils. As a soft Core man himself, one who knew the issues inside out and enjoyed the confidence of all parties, he proved a remarkably effective negotiator.

The first, or so-called bypass, amendment addressed the authority of the governing Standing Committee on the Core Program during the four-year transition period. It empowered the committee "to make evolutionary changes" in the program and requirements before the final ratification in 1983. More

specifically, it "authorized and urged" the committee to designate as substitutes for particular course requirements within
the program appropriate "Core-related sequences"—two or
more related or complementary departmental courses—that
met the same objectives. It also "encouraged" the substitution
of advanced departmental courses on a one-for-one basis. This
was a restrained version of the limited bypass proposal placed
before the Faculty Council by the student-faculty Committee
on Undergraduate Education and its Educational Resources
Group: restrained in the sense that it did not *require* the committee to permit substitutions for Core courses but only urged
it to do so if such action seemed desirable. As Rosovsky noted
later, the amendment "did not dictate an outcome."

Proponents of the amendment intended that the number of
alternative Core-related sequences should be small. While
maintaining the objectives of the program, this option would
offer a "natural status" for indivisible two-semester courses,
provide opportunities for students to explore concentration
choices, or aid those who wished to develop a minor field. The
one-for-one departmental bypass was intended to cover a
limited number of appropriate advanced offerings that might
be excluded from the short list of Core courses because their
level made them unsuitable for many students. Thus the message of the first amendment was that the Standing Committee
should not be bound by the initial structure of the program in
meeting its objectives; if supplementary strategies seemed desirable, it should be free to adopt them.

The second, or so-called floater, amendment reflected a
nagging concern that the arrangement of Core requirements
might warrant further refinement or simplification. It called
upon the Standing Committee to examine and experiment with
alternatives that would shift, or permit some or all students to
shift, one course requirement to another area, without reducing the total number of requirements. More specifically, the

committee was urged to see whether the objectives of Literature and Arts could be met by two required courses rather than three; whether one aspect of the Historical Study requirement could be worked into another area, thereby reducing the requirement in the two areas by one course; whether three rather than two course requirements might be developed to permit progression in Science and in Social Analysis and Moral Reasoning. The purpose of this amendment was to "avoid premature hardening of the categories" and to ensure further study of the desirability of an elective element within the program. Again, area objectives would remain unchanged; the issue was whether different amounts of time might be spent in meeting them.

The Council's strategy for the discussion of amendments at the April meeting was to begin with those considered pertinent to the main motion, moving from the most friendly to the most hostile. Once the proposal on the floor was amended as the faculty saw fit, a vote would be called on substitute motions, followed by a vote on the "clarified" Core program. The Council viewed the flexibility amendments as entirely friendly, but it unanimously opposed all that followed.

At the April faculty meeting, Biology Professor Otto Solbrig presented the Faculty Council's favorable view of the flexibility amendments. Drawing an elaborate analogy, he advised his colleagues that genetic mechanisms underlying morphological or anatomical structures usually consisted of two kinds of genes—structural genes and modifiers. In the course of evolution, it is the modifiers that allow the system to adjust. He saw the two amendments as the "modifier genes" of the Core Program, permitting adaptations to improve its fitness over time.

But James Q. Wilson, by now a grizzled veteran of Core debates, had a different view of the Core's evolutionary prospects. He was "reluctant to tamper with Professor Solbrig's genes," and he could not but favor any reasonable amendment that might lead the faculty to an enthusiastic endorsement of the program. He did not even oppose the literal intent of the amendments: who could object to the concept of flexibility? But if the past held any wisdom for the present, it suggested that the way was now being cleared for the deterioration of the Core concept. "All it would take for a committee—perhaps not the first committee appointed, but its successor committees composed perhaps of persons less enthusiastic, less committed, less under the watchful eye of the dean—all it would take for some committee to convert a carefully selected opportunity for flexibility into a generalized departmental bypass was for it to blink twice." The faculty, however, found Solbrig's cheerful optimism more persuasive than Wilson's dour prophecy, and with little further discussion went on to approve the first two amendments by a voice vote.

The next item, a proposal to amend the history requirement by changing the second group of courses, titled Historical Process and Perspective, to Great Traditions of Western Thought, was advocated principally by Philosophy Professor Robert Nozick. He and his supporters argued the importance of requiring students to choose at least one course dealing with the classics of Western thought, saw no place for this in the program as proposed, and did not see the need for two course requirements devoted solely to the methods and approaches of historians.

Defenders of the history area formulation did not deny the value of exposing students to classic works of Western thought. Indeed, an emphasis on key texts pervaded most of the Core program. There seemed no need to single out great traditions of thought, but if that should prove desirable at a later time, the floater amendment paved the way. Furthermore, the Historical Process and Perspective requirement had a special purpose: to take apart some complicated event and, by examining all of the intertwined elements, show students how oversimplification falsifies human experience. The faculty, caught up in a process in which the complex interplay of ideas, individual decisions, and accident were slowly shaping an outcome, paused but briefly to consider the Nozick amendment. The hour of normal adjournment was at hand, the discussion had been intense and tiring, Nozick's speech was long and abstruse at some points, and there were several items on the agenda that would have to be carried over to the next meeting. So someone called the question, which fell by a mixed show of hands.

After the April meeting, Core advocates grew confident. They believed they had broadened their base of support by re-assuring critics of their evolutionary intentions. They were committed primarily to the aims and objectives of the program and only secondarily to particular strategies for achieving them. They were not prepared to negotiate such complex issues on the floor of the faculty, and the committees they proposed were ideally suited to explore better ways of meeting the Core goals. Their endorsement of the flexibility amendments sufficed as evidence of open-mindedness. As the final regular faculty meeting in May approached, it seemed likely that the moderate critics of the Core had been won over. There re-mained the need to confront more fundamental opposition, in the form of one ostensibly friendly amendment and one sub-stitute motion.

The amendment suggested that the Core program should be "the normal method" for meeting nonconcentration require-ments, but that during the transition period before 1983 any student should be allowed to petition to replace the Core with an alternative distribution formula. This would entail a mix of introductory and advanced courses in two areas of natural sciences, social sciences, or humanities, depending on the stu-dent's concentration. The option was intended for a small number of students with exceptional preparation and ability, it was said to be "more demanding" than the Core, and it was expected that departments could supervise the option with a minimum of administrative folderol.

Despite assertions that the amendment would "strengthen" the Core program, Council members viewed it as hostile. It was flawed conceptually in that it proposed an alternative that *any* student—the least as well as the most well prepared and able—might exercise. Yet that flaw could hardly be considered inadvertent, for the entire proposal hinged upon a set of internally consistent assumptions: that specialization is the most important aim of undergraduate education, that the purpose of nonconcentration requirements is to prevent overspecialization, that the most serious courses are those mounted as part of a departmental curriculum. Most important of all, the amendment would take away from the faculty as a whole the authority for stating general education priorities and transfer it to students and their departmental advisers. This emphasis ignored the main thrust of the Core idea. Rosovsky and his colleagues were quick to perceive that if the faculty supported a mere distribution requirement, no matter how restrictive, then the Core was doomed before it started. Although the amendment appeared to provide just one more degree of curricular flexibility, they argued that it would in fact seriously alter the faculty's course. Through a decisive show of hands at the May meeting, the faculty agreed.

At this point it was clear that a strong tide was running in favor of the Core legislation. Consideration of a substitute motion to develop a program of minor concentrations was more or less perfunctory; the arguments pro and con had been heard before. Core advocates rested their case with the statesmanlike observations of Government Professor Samuel Beer. His own undergraduate education had been organized on the basis of a major and a minor, and he thought that it had then, and still had, a lot of value. He would want to entertain the possibility for Harvard if the Core curriculum did not work out. But he was not prepared to prejudge the Core, which he thought "dubious" and "tricky" yet contained "too much promise for the Faculty to give it up now." The promise lay in the creation of specially designed courses for nonconcentrators— "an idea not at all common in American education, and one that is more and more important." Beer thought the key question was who would teach the courses. He urged the dean to "beat the bushes, scour the countryside, cast pearls before swine, do whatever is necessary to get those courses!"

At last Rosovsky reintroduced the Core legislation, stressing that it was designed to allow the conduct of a "carefully controlled experiment." He believed that serious problems inevitably would arise during its implementation, but he thought they could be surmounted if the faculty's commitment matched his own. He asked that every vote in favor signify "more than passive acquiescence." When the hands were counted, 182 faculty members were in favor and 65 opposed.

To be sure, there were a variety of factors influencing those 247 individual decisions. Each member of the faculty had to sort out his reactions to specific details of the proposal, to its general thrust, and to the choice of arguments and style of Core advocates and their critics. Was there enough science and mathematics, or too much? Had the great books and important traditions of thought been sacrificed to excessive disciplinary self-consciousness? Were the guidelines sufficiently inclusive? Were all the negotiations and compromises that went into the final packaging of the Core proposal political in the good sense or in the bad sense? Did the plan envision a genuine refurnishing of the curriculum or only a modest moving around of the old furniture? And what of Rosovsky's active role in guiding the reforms through the faculty? Was he drawing on his personal popularity to make this a vote of confidence in his deanship? It was widely known that he had recently refused the presidency of a prominent Ivy League university, in large part because he felt he could not walk out on his commitment to the Core reform. Could the faculty do less than respond in kind?

But in the moment of decision, individual faculty members also had to answer to their own beliefs about the aims of undergraduate education, the nature and intellectual needs of students, and the character of their responsibility for the transmission of knowledge. By a sizable majority they appear to have concluded that it was as important to set a standard of intellectual range for all students as it was to require that they concentrate on a particular subject that engaged their interests. Moreover, they appear to have agreed that the range should be defined in terms of a set of essential skills and ways of thinking that could offer students some degree of leverage—a starting point for discovering, organizing, and understanding—on the knowledge they would need or want to acquire in their later lives. A sizable majority also apparently believed that all students, no matter how diversely prepared and motivated, were capable of reaching and benefiting from this intellectual standard. And finally, by almost three to one, the voting members of the Faculty of Arts and Sciences appeared to believe that, no matter how specialized their expertise, they were responsible for and capable of upholding that standard.

4

The Politics of
Curricular Reform

A three-to-one faculty majority in favor of a highly structured program of general education would have been unimaginable in the generation of the 1950s and 1960s. At the peak of the postwar expansion of universities, the idea of regulatory standards for undergraduate education came to seem perverse. New subjects and advanced work were all the rage. Indeed, the call for more options—"innovative" subjects, interdisciplinary approaches, research seminars for freshmen, and self-designed majors for sophomores—extended well beyond the content of the curriculum to its very structure. The older system of course examinations and grading gave way to a growing number of wild cards that allowed students course credit for independent, unsupervised work. The loosening of the system encouraged students to place out of the freshman year and to interrupt their studies for a period of wandering in the Great World. Growing opportunities to pursue advanced work and esoteric interests were accompanied by a decline in the proportion of basic undergraduate course offerings.

This new conventional wisdom of curricular flexibility, variety, and choice—which became a hallmark of the American multiversity—led to near chaos by the late 1960s. It was not, after all, the product of a coherent educational philosophy but rather the sum of piecemeal, special-interest reforms. These were designed, in the first instance, by faculty members who wanted to ease the burden of general requirements on the ablest students so that they might concentrate on advanced work. These changes were followed by student-initiated reforms that democratized access to exemption privileges and thus liberated everyone from the constraints imposed by standardized requirements. There seemed to be no common understanding among a highly professionalized faculty as to what could or should be expected of an undergraduate population that was diverse in abilities, preparation, and interests. Nor, as time wore on, did the faculty seem inclined even to consider this question.

One major difficulty was that what Clark Kerr in 1963 called a "pluralist institution" had become, six years later, an ungoverned one. Who was to say what curricular standards and priorities should obtain? It was a time of faculty querulousness and divisiveness. Political factions on all sides leaped to attack any suggestion for change. Rosovsky likened the prevailing attitude to that of the country at large when he observed that "any program will be criticized from the left and from the right for all the usual reasons; in all probability it will also face carping words from the center because of a presumed right or left slant."

It was not inevitable that Harvard emerged relatively quickly from this disabling condition in the 1970s. But at least two elements worked in the university's favor: a long tradition of conservative financial management and, ironically, its unequivocal commitment to faculty self-governance. In the 1970s financial retrenchment became the preoccupation of most American universities, but Harvard felt the pinch early —not because its resources were unusually or uniquely strained but because, like the Boston heiress who turned to prostitution, it did not believe in dipping into capital. So some way had to be found, short of taking to the streets, for making decisions about institutional priorities. This is not to say that educational reform was simply the product of cost-mindedness, any more than social change in the 1960s was simply the result of political activism. But the new, fiscally inspired stress on priorities was an important element in launching the movement for coherent educational reform.

Faculty self-governance is a value scarcely unique to Harvard, though it is guarded there with ferocious jealousy. And under ordinary circumstances this fact of life is a major obstacle to decision making. As James Q. Wilson has observed, "The faculty is supposed to govern collegially but it is not a collegium." The Harvard faculty is, in fact, a collection of scholars and teachers who define themselves first in terms of their professional expertise. That is why research and departmental instruction, especially at the graduate level, have a much higher place in the concerns of most faculty members than does the general or nonspecialized education of undergraduates. Nevertheless, as scholars and teachers, the faculty exercises guardianship over the entire Harvard College curriculum. No one, least of all Rosovsky, contested the faculty's position as head of the household. Indeed, his initial critique of undergraduate education in 1974 was deliberately designed to stir his colleagues' dormant sense of collective responsibility.

Rosovsky thoroughly understood that the key issue was not whether he could persuade enough faculty members to go along with the administration's initiatives, but whether the faculty had the *capacity* to arrive at a consensus. Unless there was some common ground of experience and conviction to sustain an educational standard, reform was pointless. Consequently he saw his role as engaging the largest possible number of his colleagues in the process of identifying what he termed "simple, operational and widely acceptable goals." In short, he took the position that the only workable solution would be one that emerged from the faculty itself. Hence the four years of arduous consensus building, which involved so many consultations and internal debates, so many explications and revisions, so much bargaining over details and nuances of language. What may have appeared to outsiders as a mere "patchwork of compromises" was, however flawed or unconventional, a conception of general education rooted in the experiences and values of the scholars and teachers who committed themselves to it.

Reactions: Critical Constituencies Within and Without

The first hurdle—convincing the faculty that there was a problem requiring collective attention—was the easiest, though it was not without hazards. In his initial communication to the faculty, Rosovsky offered an inventory of the warts and blemishes that marred the Harvard undergraduate program. But while the faculty's self-ciritical bent was stimulated by Rosovsky's fire, numerous friends and institutional rivals of Harvard also were exercised by his candor. Some loyal alumni active in fund-raising activities were taken aback by the spirited display of self-criticism: was it really necessary to flaunt dirty laundry in the window? Does Macy's tell Gimbel's? And some of Harvard's rivals, though they experienced most of the same problems, were all too ready to imply that their own institutions were different. From the beginning, the uninvited interest of the national media strained the mood at Harvard in another way. Local and national newspapers, exhibiting their special talent for magnifying every sneeze into a plague, flashed the news that Harvard had isolated the cause of ignorance. Feeling exposed and slightly ridiculous, the faculty resented what it viewed as a coercive buildup of expectations.

Some faculty members read the story of the unraveling of

the older General Education Program as a cautionary tale. It demonstrated, they thought, the impossibility of maintaining standards of education outside the confines of departmental concentrations and Ph.D. programs. Still, few faculty members believed that students would use a sizable amount of free choice well. And they did not view increased specialization as a real alternative. Most professors were unwilling to abandon the idea of general education, however nebulous it had become. To be sure, there were deep divisions over the nature and scope of requirements, but the issue quickly centered on the question, what sort of intellectual breadth is useful?

Utility had always been an underlying theme of the general education movement, which had as its first goal the creation of an informed and responsible citizenry. Now, however, the emphasis shifted from a common learning to a standard of intellectual competence, from a basic portfolio of blue-chip knowledge to a diversified holding of intellectual growth stocks. The point was to expose students to a range of intellectual enterprises in order to extend their capacity to absorb or extract knowledge. The psychologist Roger Brown spoke for the new emphasis on individual rather than social utility when he observed that "the benefits to the individual of being moved around a little so that he will discover early what he is able to do and what interests him enough to matter in his life is as important to me as the social goals of 'common discourse' and the 'educated citizen.' " As the Core took shape, most onlookers were surprised by the degree to which faculty reactions cut across departmental lines. And the reality of consensus was underscored by the fact that despite sharp disagreements over details, the broad outline of the Core remained strikingly stable through innumerable revisions.

Yet once the faculty reached agreement in principle on the need for, and the character of, a Core Curriculum, departmental interest groups began to voice their concerns. Rosovsky described this as the "where is mine?" phase. It started when a few highly specialized faculty members working in fields (such as linguistics) peripheral to the mainstream of undergraduate education sought assurances that they would be included in the new program. Rosovsky thought it odd that these colleagues should wish to be included in a scheme defined with reference to "basic general education." He certainly would not propose his own specialized work in Japanese economic history as suitable for the Core. But there were realistic grounds for anxiety that the new program would draw financial resources away from other activities, and those who taught specialized undergraduate courses to a very few students inevitably felt vulnerable.

Numerically, the most significant group of internal critics was the scientists, primarily those in the physical and applied sciences, and mathematicians. The issue for them was more complicated than the mere protection of turf. Many were dubious in principle about the need and value of a Core program. On the whole, scientists tend to see in their classrooms students with superior training and versatile minds—the very students who are best equipped and most likely to venture into other areas of the curriculum. Thus many saw no burning need for a mandatory program of general education. They also worried about the impact of such a requirement on Harvard's attraction for well-prepared students.

A subset of scientists and mathematicians focused their attention on the "other half" of the undergraduate population—the mass of students who had not achieved, or would not or could not achieve, a sufficient level of quantitative skills. Among this faculty group there was a split between those who believed that *any* general education designed for such a group was bound to be "unserious" and those who believed that general education in "real science" was not only essential but far too complex and important to be administered in small doses. The two-course requirement formulated in the Core plan struck the one side as unecessary and the other as inadequate.

On the failings of the status quo, student opinion was as nearly unanimous as the faculty's. But from the outset the student press—still imbued with the visceral hostility to authority of the 1960s—took an adversary stance toward the Core Curriculum. With some exceptions, feature, news, and editorial writers (it was often impossible to distinguish among them) viewed the Core as a paternalistic attempt "to remove the right of the individual student to structure his or her education." This attitude called for some intellectual somersaulting, since the student press had often criticized the faculty for not caring about undergraduate education and had found fault with General Education requirements not because they existed but because they lacked a rationale. "While the Gen. Ed. program certainly merited revamping," declared a *Crimson* editorial, "the Core is not the answer." The paper's editorialists held that the Core represented "a disturbing move away from the cherished, traditional concept of 'liberal education' "—a term they defined rather idiosyncratically as the freedom of students "to gain what they see as a balanced education."

The issue of student rights was an important one to campus news writers, who persistently interpreted the Core in terms of a class struggle between student masses and the faculty-administration elite. "Counter-Revolution at Harvard," screamed a headline in the *Crimson* on May 16, 1978. It seemed that the Core Curriculum, "rushed through with eleven minutes of debate on the proposal itself, and passed in spite of strong and broad-based student opposition," was only one example of "an unstated philosophy—clamp down on students—that has spread surreptitiously throughout the ranks of those who run this university." Several weeks later a more mild-mannered editorial writer chastised Harvard administrators for their failure to consult students: "True to form, the Core has arrived with a minimum of student input. It is strangely presumptuous —almost insulting—to ask undergraduates to buy the idea that a small number of Faculty members know enough about Harvard's problems to be able to suggest a replacement for Gen. Ed." Indeed, the manifest "erosion of student rights" drove one writer to announce that the message of the Core to students was "Welcome to high school."

With uncharacteristic impatience, Rosovsky observed at one point that the student press "managed to spread a considerable amount of what in intelligence circles is known as 'disinformation.' " He was referring, in part, to constant allegations that the Core was shrouded in secrecy and that student viewpoints had been systematically excluded from the debate. Attempting to remedy the faculty's ignorance of student opinion, *Crimson* staffers conducted a telephone survey of 175 randomly selected students in early April 1978. They found that 20 percent of those canvassed were not familiar with the proposals, and another 8 percent had "no opinion." But of those who said they knew about the Core, 65 percent were opposed to it.

This negative assessment was not confirmed by student representatives elected or appointed to the various committees reviewing Core proposals. On the whole these students supported the attempt to devise a more structured general curriculum. But at the same time they persistently advocated their constituency's interest in maximum flexibility and in student participation in curricular planning and governance. For the most part, the faculty discounted *Crimson* critics and took seriously the views of student representatives, adopting most— though not all—of their modifying suggestions.

It is difficult to judge which group—the *Crimson* poll or student representatives—more accurately reflected majority undergraduate opinion. Many students seemed not to be well informed about the issues, although all the reports were widely circulated and a number of Core planners made a point of meeting with groups of students in the residential houses. It was always clear that Core legislation would not be retroactive, so perhaps the fact that it would not apply to them accounted for some of the student disinterest. True, "thousands" of students—the figures of 1,800 and 2,500 were cited on separate occasions—signed a petition urging postponement of faculty action at a late stage of the 1978 debate. But this scarcely constituted evidence of widespread opposition. Since intense discussion spilled over two years, at least half of the student population was not there at the beginning and might reasonably view the pressure for closure as hasty. It must also be said that in those years "thousands" of students often signed petitions on the ground that they had no clearly formed objection to them.[1]

The passage of Core legislation in the spring of 1978 was followed by a flood of laudatory reactions in the national press, which celebrated the "stiffening" and "toughening" of academic standards. This publicity triggered a series of critical attacks, largely from educators at other institutions, many of whom had some former Harvard connection. The most impassioned assaults came from what might be described as purists. Educational perfectionists of either conservative or radical persuasions tended to agree on two main points: that intellectual standards are inherently elitist and that in a corrupt world any agreement must represent a sellout of something to someone.

Writing in the *Atlantic* (September 1978), Alston Chase, former chairman of the department of philosophy at Macalester College and a graduate of Harvard College, mourned the loss of belief in a central body of knowledge and values, which, he thought, had formed the core of intellectual life in the postwar (1945-1960) golden age of meritocracy at Harvard. Chase found the contemporary academy dominated by a new egalitarianism of ideas and interests that was "antithetical to quality education" and to "genuine educational reform." In this politicized environment, social scientists inevitably came to the fore as experts in the black art of value neutrality. They were, in effect, people without principle or loyalties who stood ready to sacrifice all values for any outcome that could be proclaimed a success. It was therefore "not surprising" that social scientists were the architects and builders of Harvard's Core Curriculum. "Their high profile," he asserted, "demonstrates that, as there is little consensus on the question of priorities, the contemporary academy perceives that its major problems are still political ones."

In *Commentary* (September 1978), a former Harvard professor of English, Kenneth Lynn, indicted his erstwhile colleagues for their failure to devise a more philosophically coherent and prescriptive curriculum, one reflecting the intellectual rapport that ought to characterize a respectable faculty. Totally lacking "a spirit of common enterprise" and fundamentally indifferent to undergraduate education, they had instead created a "Son of Gen Ed," which replicated the "insufficiently serious" features of its 1950s predecessor. A Harvard College undergraduate named Peter Engel, writing in the *Washington Monthly* (January 1980), followed suit by explaining the Core reform as "an elaborate ruse to avoid facing the fact that there are few professors at Harvard who are willing to teach an introductory blockbuster like Western Thought and Institutions . . . only a lot of professors willing to expatiate on their specialty." In sum, the conservative case was that the Core lacked a grand vision of intellectual culture; it was so scarred by compromises that it represented at worst no change at all, at best a change scarcely worth making.

Writing from a radical perspective in *Change Magazine*

(September 1978), Barry O'Connell, associate professor of American studies and English at Amherst College and a well-known political activist in his graduate student days at Harvard in the late 1960s, saw the Harvard faculty not as selfish and self-interested but as servile bureaucrats of the social order. In his scenario the Core plan concealed a hidden agenda: namely, preparing the young to accept the prevailing social, economic, and cultural conditions of American life. It was a continuation of "the war against the young" of the 1960s, when radical students rose to challenge the universities' preoccupation with licensing upward social mobility and serving power centers in government and industry. At that time students had been beguiled by apparently responsive reforms that loosened academic requirements and removed constraints on their extracurricular lives. But in the end those reforms only confirmed the function of universities as "purveyors of credentials and technical knowledge." What was wanted, according to O'Connell, was to transform the university into an adversary of the social order and an agent of constructive social change. But "Harvard's conception of the essentials of a good education in 1978 is limited to subjects most scholars in 1900 would have regarded as the Core." Moreover, the new curriculum was a deliberate move to head off further trouble from the present generation of "deeply troubled" students by appealing to their natural concern about their professional futures. It was basically a design to increase "some students' competitive edge in the mobility race," and to encourage vocationalism by asserting the material advantage of general education. The very idea that general education should serve individual, as against social, purposes seemed to confirm Harvard's philistine belief that the aim of education is worldly success.

Several months after the passage of Core legislation, some government officials, at the behest of Jimmy Carter's domestic policy staff, summoned to Washington a varied group of academic leaders from all parts of the country to construct an agenda for a future White House parley on national curricular priorities for "liberal learning in the 1980s and beyond." But many of those at the Washington conference considered any attempt to set a standard for liberal learning as a conspiracy in restraint of trade. The most vocal among them viewed such a suggestion as part of a reactionary "back to basics" impulse— to traditional subjects and academic skills—that would exclude "new learners," people whose age, background, and interests are not typical of those who have gone to college in the past, and newer fields of speculation such as women's, Black, and other ethnic studies; and educational innovations such as self-designed programs, nonclassroom learning, and community service projects. At best, the arguments of the conference participants celebrated the diversity of students' interests and aptitudes and expressed a genuine compassion for "the formerly bypassed." At worst, they were a set of variations on the theme "where is mine?"

Most striking was the assumption of many conferees that education is a "client-centered" business. It was the obligation of educators, they held, to ensure the widest possible array of services and the broadest possible availability to their students. In this company it was open season on "professors who only care about their own thing," on that repository of villainy the academic department, on core curricula in general, and on Harvard in particular for attempting to "corner the credentialing market and lock everybody else out." The Core, it seemed, was a kind of pedagogical Proposition 13, imposing narrowly defined limits on educational services. After two days of vox populism, the government officials at the conference quietly reformulated their goal as "legitimizing diversity in the solving of common problems" and abandoned their plans for a White House parley.

So on the whole, both radical and liberal critics in effect accepted the conservative argument that intellectual standards are inherently elitist—only they found Harvard's standards too exclusionary and authoritarian, while the conservatives found them too trendy and egalitarian.

Many external reactions to the Core were not so much critiques as exercises in the deflation of Harvard hubris. Some commentators saw it as a mere "relabeling of old-fashioned General Education." And in those few quarters where older prescriptive programs still retained some of their potency, Harvard's action was hailed as the return of a prodigal son to the fold. "Harvard rediscovers U. of C.'s 'core' plan," claimed a headline writer for the *Chicago Tribune*. Others, noting that there were to be between eighty and one hundred courses in the Core program, observed that Harvard had vindicated student choice as the basic organizing principle of the curriculum. "The emperor has no clothes," declared Adele Simmons, president of Hampshire College; the Core, it seemed, was rotten. After visiting his alma mater in the spring of 1981, Timothy Foote, a senior editor of *Time*, opined: "The Core is a misnomer. The principle of General Education seems dead at Harvard. In its place is a glorious delicatessen." These interpretations assumed that a Core Curriculum must require all students to take identical courses. For some it strained credulity to claim that name for a curriculum that permitted students to choose among a limited number of courses designed to meet the same educational objectives.

In yet another interpretation the program was seen as a directed sampling of specialized departmental courses—just a fancy-dress way for faculty to continue teaching "their own thing." This view was commonly held by those who bemoaned the apparent consignment of the great books and great ideas to a subordinate or instrumental role. Like many of the conservative critics, these people thought that the opportunity to recreate a common culture based on shared books and values had been lost. But many educators who had no particular bias in favor of an alternative formulation of general education were genuinely puzzled by the first list of Core courses that appeared in 1979. Offerings such as The Russian Revolution, International Conflicts in the Modern World, Culture and Human Development, and Modern Physics: Concepts and Development, to select a few titles at random, seemed to be either small-scale surveys or to fit easily into departmental curricula. What was special about these courses that qualified them for inclusion in the Core Curriculum? And if the courses were not distinctive, then how did the Core differ from a set of distribution requirements over departmental offerings?

Thus critics besieged the Core from all sides. It was too elitist and insufficiently elitist; it was back to basics and a delicatessen; it was old-fashioned General Education and a frivolous distortion of it, replacing substance with bureaucracy; it was an authoritarian statement and a patchwork of compromises; it was too narrowly specialized and not sharply enough focused on certain books and ideas; it was counterrevolutionary, yet it represented no change at all; it transferred all power to departments while vindicating student choice.

The home team found these criticisms exasperating. Defensively, James Q. Wilson wrote in an article, titled "Harvard's Core Curriculum: A View From the Inside," in *Change Magazine* (November 1978) that

> there is nothing most of us would like better than to be left alone in this enterprise—not because we have no use for criticism, but because we do not see Harvard as a model for what all colleges ought to be. Believing in the virtues of educational diversity, convinced that colleges have begun to acquire a dulling sameness in their curricula, and knowing that what is possible in one place may be (for reasons of tradition, organization, or finances) impossible or undesirable in another, we have avoided issuing manifestos or claiming any special virtue.

Yet willy-nilly, Harvard had been "cast in the role of examplar." Critics acted as though Harvard "ought to represent the ideal." But since each critic had a different ideal, Harvard was always found wanting. Moreover, Wilson argued, the views expressed by outside critics had been "ardently and forcefully expressed by one or more professors or students who were part of Harvard's self-examination." Internal debate had not suffered from a lack of opposing views about the purposes of higher education. Indeed, there had been "dozens of conflicts, large and small, in the preferences of the several hundred members of the Faculty of Arts and Sciences who eventually played some role in shaping the final decision." He wondered "what method, other than hand-to-hand combat" the critics themselves would have used to determine which views ought to prevail.

Wilson was not alone in believing that the "more striking" aspect of the process of reform was the "extent and durability of the agreement on the broad outlines" of the Core and on the subjects that ought to be included in it. One could argue that in a certain sense Harvard had merely reaffirmed its post-World War II commitment to a separate program of general education that would develop courses for its own purposes and redirect the effort of teachers to basic undergraduate instruction.

Had that been all that was achieved, perhaps debate would have been a little less intense and protracted, and the fact of agreement less noteworthy. But the practical details of the Core amounted to a departure from past practice. To begin with, the list of subjects included several that had not been required before: quantitative reasoning, foreign cultures, music and fine arts, moral reasoning, and "hard" science. The three most innovative inclusions—quantitative reasoning, with its emphasis on data analysis and the use of computers; foreign cultures, reflecting the postwar growth of interest in other societies and in understanding American society from the outside, so to speak; and moral reasoning—each constituted a response to changing societal needs and values.

Perhaps the most striking symbol of adaptation of contemporary realities was the moral reasoning requirement. In the nineteenth century a course in Moral Philosophy was required of all seniors in Harvard College, embodying one of the primary goals of the college curriculum before 1870: to promote the Christian religion. In its contemporary reincarnation, this requirement continued to reflect the influence of the surrounding society—except that it no longer aimed to promote the particular view of one dominant group but rather to teach students to make rational choices among the competing values defined by groups of equal standing within a pluralist society.

Moreover, the distinguishing feature of the Core was not so much the required subjects as the way in which they were to be treated. If one looks at the titles of Core courses (see the Appendix), it is not immediately apparent how they differ from routine departmental fare. To be sure, many of the courses can fulfill departmental objectives as well as the purposes of the Core. A satisfactory offering in, for example, Literature and Arts, or Historical Study, could hardly fail to be valuable as well to the relevant department. But the converse is *not* true. Even if as many as 60 to 80 percent of Core offerings were useful as departmental courses, a far smaller proportion of departmental courses would satisfy the particular objectives of the Core areas. To illustrate: the History Department might well offer a course on the history of modern China but for such a course to qualify for the Core, the material would have to be selected and organized to focus on some significant feature of the contemporary world such as the adaptation of traditional societies to modernity, using China as a case study and making relevant comparisons.

The primary pedagogical intention of Core courses is to introduce students to the kinds of analysis peculiar to certain disciplines and the problems to which they are typically applied. The topics treated are in the nature of case materials: ideally, they are important, interesting, and diverse. But no matter how varied the case materials, every course in a given Core area has the same pedagogical purpose. Rosovsky's favorite illustration of the principle supposes the adoption of a requirement in martial arts for the purposes of teaching physical fitness and self-defense. That purpose could be achieved equally by a course in karate, kung fu, aikido, or tai chi. The point is simply that courses in each area are equivalent to each other in methodological emphasis and educational aim. In this respect the Core continues to promote the "common learning" aspect of general education. But the character of that learning has shifted from a predetermined body of knowledge to a specific set of skills and modes of thought.

Starting Up The Core

According to its construction plans, the Core program would need four years for full implementation. The eight-course requirement would not come into effect until the fall of 1982, thereby allowing time for the development of a full set of offerings in each area and the resolution of issues left pending at the conclusion of faculty debate. Only then could the experiment begin to be judged.

In the 1978-79 academic year the Core committees started to generate and approve the initial list of courses, from which students entering in the fall of 1979 would have to select two. Despite all that had gone before, it was a year of groping uncertainty, as fifty-four faculty members and sixteen students on eight different committees tackled the practical problems of transforming wishes into deeds.

The committees faced an unprecedented task. Unlike the

typical college-wide curriculum review committee, they were not simply obliged to judge whether or not a course proposal was "good." They also had to evaluate each proposal according to specific criteria set forth in the area guidelines, which required thoughtful interpretation by committee members and considerable willingness to adjust on the part of those teaching the courses. Each proposal was subject to double scrutiny, first by area subcommittees and then by the watchdog Standing Committee, composed of the area chairmen. In addition, the committees were expected not merely to review but also to recruit course proposals with an eye toward balancing the offerings in each area.

Whether by virtue of faculty enthusiasm or the aggressiveness of Core recruiters, no fewer than 125 course proposals were submitted during the first year. Twenty were rejected because they did not fit the guidelines. A slightly larger number were put on hold while instructors considered changes recommended by committee members. Fifty-five were accepted for the fall of 1979 and an additional twenty-nine for the following year. Of these eighty-four approved courses, fifty-three were created especially for the Core program—the largest single injection of new undergraduate courses in anyone's memory. Twenty-four were extensively altered versions of existing courses, and seven were straightforward transplants, mainly from the General Education Program. Rosovsky and his colleagues proclaimed that this number exceeded their most optimistic hopes and pointed with manifest pride to the very substantial number of distinguished scholars and teachers who had signed up.

Inevitably the pace of course development slackened after the first year. Routine cancellations reduced the base figure so that the listing for 1980-81 showed a net gain of only thirteen courses. More troublesome was the uneven growth of area listings. Molecular biologists resisted Rosovsky's blandishments, and some historians were not enthusiastic about the idiosyncratic formulation of Historical Study. Most surprising was the complete reversal of expectations within the area of Literature and Arts. No one thought there would be any difficulty in securing an ample number of genre courses in literature, fine arts, and music; many were skeptical about the interdisciplinary prescription for courses in contexts of culture. But the latter grouping attracted a flood of proposals, often diverting faculty interest from the more discipline-based offerings.

Courses in moral reasoning followed the overall pattern: a quick start tapering off to slow growth. This result was fully expected, for there were only a few philosophers and political theorists in Arts and Sciences departments whose interests lent themselves to the Core's objectives. Fortunately, several members of the law faculty who had taught before in the General Education Program were eager to adapt their courses to the new format.

An early test of the faculty's determination to uphold its newly formulated standards came with the implementation of the quantitative reasoning requirement. Some faculty members and admissions officers had been quietly critical of the view widely prevalent at Harvard College (as at other Ivy League schools and Oxford and Cambridge as well) that once a student was admitted he or she should be "gotten through." This view was reflected in the provision for medical exemptions from foreign language study and in the toleration of well-known "gut" courses. Fred Jewett, dean of admissions, thought that such leniency undercut his efforts to uphold academic standards in admissions. No sooner was the quantitative reasoning requirement put in place in the fall of 1980 than he received some protests from the parents of new freshmen who claimed that their offspring were being discriminated against. They advised Jewett that there were, after all, laws protecting the handicapped. Cynics among the faculty wondered how long it would be before someone with appropriate credentials invented an organic inability to do numbers called "discalculia," which would provide the basis for medical exemptions. But the Standing Committee on the Core moved quickly to head off pressure on behalf of "hardship" cases by issuing a flat warning that no student would be eligible for the bachelor's degree without meeting the quantitative reasoning requirement. By June 1981, 88 percent of the freshmen class had done so, and another 10 percent had passed at least one of two mandatory examinations on the use of the computer and the interpretation of data.

Meanwhile, the Standing Committee turned its attention to some thorny administrative decisions, dubbed "sleepers" because of their long-term impact—and their capacity to induce boredom. Students were to receive exemptions from two of the ten Core subareas covered by their departmental concentrations. In most cases it was clear which Core exemptions were appropriate to each field of concentration. English literature majors, for example, would not be required to take Core courses in Literature or Contexts of Culture. But some majors, philosophy, for example, seemed to have only one Core equivalent. In these cases the Committee agreed to give students the option of taking a second exemption in any area except science, anticipating that many students would avoid science if they were free to do so.

An important expression of the Standing Committee's relatively hard-line approach was its resolution of the pass/fail issue. The committee consulted each of its subcommittees, with indeterminate results. It listened intently to the case made by the student-faculty Committee on Undergraduate Education for allowing students to use the pass/fail option in two out of eight Core courses. The basic argument was the one that had given rise to pass/fail in the 1960s: that it would encourage students to take a flier on a course far removed from their field of interest or academic strength.

The committee was not convinced. It might well make sense to encourage students to take "difficult" courses as electives, but it seemed absurd to argue that in *required* areas they should be so induced. And the committee found an unresolved contradiction in the view that some students were both fearful and willing to stretch. The more likely usage of the pass/fail option by risk-averse students would be to protect themselves from even the minimum standards imposed by the program. Conversely, venturesome students, by definition, did not need any insurance against risk.

A more complex issue was that of designating advanced departmental courses or Core-related sequences as substitutes for particular Core requirements. The Standing Committee had been "authorized and urged" to make such designations, primarily for courses in the science departments, and the Science subcommittee set about preparing a list of advanced courses that met Core objectives. But the Standing Committee determined to resist awarding Core credit for advanced departmental courses in other areas on the ground that it could not scrutinize the content and conduct of such offerings with the same thoroughness it applied to the Core courses. They felt that other considerations, such as the possibly adverse impact of numerous departmental bypasses on the development of Core courses and their potential for relieving enrollment pressure on Core courses, tended to cancel each other out. Still, the possiblity of substituting Core-related sequences was left open for student petition on the ground that there might well be cases—say, where students made a late shift in their field of concentration—requiring a measure of flexibility.

No issue wracked the Standing Committee more than the question of quality control. When recommending a proposed course, each subcommittee was asked to comment on the teaching effectiveness of the instructor. Although some of the subcommittees were reluctant to do so, it was usually possible to identify instructors whose teaching skills, or lack thereof, suggested that they would not be successful as instructors in the Core. It was also relatively easy to predict the future stars of the program. But there remained a large group of instructors about whom little was known, either because they were new or because they had never before taught undergraduate lecture courses of this type. As a recruiting agency, the Standing Committee had no choice but to take calculated risks. Some of the unknowns were bound to prove less than satisfactory, so the question then was, how to make such judgments and what to do about them?

The larger undergraduate courses at Harvard are elaborately described and rated in an annual *Course Evaluation Guide* prepared by students with some faculty supervision and subsidy. The basis of evaluation is a questionnaire distributed, with the instructor's permission, to all students in a given course. Some older faculty members object passionately to this publication, which they view as an encouragement to "consumerism," but on the whole it has gained acceptance and respect. Nevertheless, to meet faculty objections to the *Guide*, the Standing Committee was willing to prepare its own student surveys for the sole purpose of providing information to instructors and to Core subcommittees. Core administrators also would interview instructors and teaching assistants to get their views on the strengths and weaknesses of their courses.

The discussion of various ways to evaluate Core courses proceeded amiably enough until James Q. Wilson, chairman of the subcommittee on Social Analysis and Moral Reasoning, reported that his colleagues had decided to visit every course offered in their area. The clear implication was that for these courses, evaluation in one form or another would no longer require an instructor's permission; it was to be mandatory.

The form of active supervision proposed by Wilson's subcommittee led to the first split in the Standing Committee. Those who opposed evaluation in any form—arguing, essentially, that professors have a right to teach as they choose—had been willing to go along with a scheme that depended on an instructor's consent. But they could not accept evaluation without consent. Their opponents countered that the right to teach was not at issue: instructors deemed unsuitable for Core teaching could take their courses to departments or to other sponsoring agencies. They believed that the case for evaluating Core courses was so reasonable that the overwhelming majority of instructors would subscribe to it voluntarily. As for those who did not, some sacrifice of faculty liberty was a small price to pay for the ensuing benefit to the college. In the end, the Standing Committee maintained that Core courses would have to be evaluated, though each subcommittee might choose its own means. While this outcome seemed in retrospect to be inevitable, the discussion bore a striking resemblance to the 1978 debate on Core legislation, in that it was charged with strong feelings and would not have come out the same way a generation earlier.

In 1978 Derek Bok likened the task of reforming the curriculum to that of "moving a cemetery." His lugubrious image applied with equal cogency to the planning and implementation stages. Seven years after Rosovsky's initial call for a review of undergraduate education at Harvard, it is possible only to give an interim progress report on the Core. In the academic year 1981-82 freshmen needed to meet only three-quarters of the requirements. At present, the program is enjoying the benefit of a Hawthorne effect: it is new, the dean and the president are solidly behind it, and it represents a dramatic change from what was done in the past. A substantial number of faculty members have come forward with new courses, and many of them exhibit a missionary zeal in their Core teaching. Students appear to be flocking to the courses—in 1981-82 there were about 50 percent more enrollments than were required, indicating that a large number of students were taking Core courses as electives.

But it is too early to tell whether the faculty's current enthusiasm will sustain itself over time, and there is no way to judge the impact of the Core on undergraduates, because the transition stage has all of the flexibility, and some of the incoherence, of the older General Education Program. Indeed, it will not be possible to measure the full impact of the Core—whether its aims are achieved and how it fits together with other components of undergraduate education—until 1986, when the first class of students entering under the new arrangement is graduated.

Two difficulties, both anticipated, have already come to the fore. A few of the science professors who have newly joined the program are discovering how difficult and frustrating it can be to teach "hard" science to nonscientists. In the General Education Program this problem finally led to softening the courses. The situation will worsen after 1982, when it will no longer be possible for any student to avoid the science courses. Some instructors have added extra sessions in mathematical techniques to their courses, but it remains to be seen whether a sufficient number of science teachers will find ways to maintain the new standards.

The second problem has to do with the strain on teaching resources and facilities, especially for the new requirements in art and music. In order to provide their share of Core instructors, many departments have begun to reorganize their undergraduate and graduate programs, pruning, consolidating, and offering specialized courses with low enrollments in alternate years. But the new pattern of course taking dictated by full implementation of the Core program inevitably will require a significant reallocation of teaching resources to Core areas.[2] The Core's demands on audiovisual equipment and classroom facilities already have exceeded expectations, forcing the administration to be more responsible about providing instructional support services than had been the case.

Other dilemmas have begun to appear on the agenda of the Standing Committee and its subcommittees: how to maintain a balanced offering of subjects in each area with the limited (and changing) pool of teachers available each year; how to ensure sufficient variation in the level of difficulty of Core courses so that all are not too elementary for upperclassmen and well-prepared freshmen or, far more likely, too advanced for the average freshman; how to keep a balance in enrollments such that courses are not too small to hold a place among the deliberately limited number of offerings in each area or too large for teachers to manage; how to set and maintain a high standard of instruction in the discussion sections led predominantly by graduate student teaching assistants.

Still, one can point to several incontrovertible achievements. The Core program has mounted an impressive number of interesting and attractive new courses for nonconcentrators that would not otherwise have come into being. It has established a coherent framework for student course selection and justified requirements in terms of contemporary students' intellectual needs. The debate that preceded it clarified the goals of undergraduate education for faculty and students alike. Moreover, the seemingly interminable process of establishing the Core has gone some considerable way to redress the slippage of concern for undergraduate education that was one of the less seemly consequences of what Kenneth Lynn has called "the go-go years of Harvard growth" in the 1950s and 1960s.[3]

Indeed, it can be argued that the single most important decision in connection with the Core was Rosovsky's choice of a strategy for change. From the outset he insisted that educational reform was a collective responsibility of the faculty and not merely "an administrative assignment." In large part, his decision to engage the maximum number of participants derived from his personal style and temperament and his unwavering belief in Harvard as an institution. Once convinced of the need for reform, he concentrated his boundless energy on that task. His avuncular, modest, and noncompetitive manner enabled him to enlist as loyal lieutenants strong and independent-minded colleagues who did not always agree with his views or decisions. His candor and willingness to listen often took the edge off hostile criticism.

Some said Rosovsky was fair-minded to a fault; others, that he put the faculty under relentless pressure. But the prevailing impression was of a man firmly in charge, fully committed and yet flexible. Indeed, he often described himself with the supposedly Napoleonic aphorism, "On s'engage et puis on voit." Thus he could comfortably tolerate the contradiction, more apparent than real, between his belief that there were certain things every educated person should know and his endorsement of a plan "that is not cast in concrete." Determined to talk out the issues until he had a consensus, he managed to elicit not agreement on every detail—that would have been asking the impossible—but movement in a common direction. Yet even Rosovsky's extraordinary devotion to reform might not have been sufficient without the consistent and visible support of President Derek Bok, the sustained commitment of James Q. Wilson, and the readiness of more than a dozen other influential senior faculty members to shoulder the burden of planning and persuasion at critical junctures.

Whether or not Harvard's Core program ultimately succeeds, the ideas and controversies behind it stem from important characteristics of American academic life in the 1970s. Harvard College may be unique in many respects, but it shares with other liberal arts schools a set of social and academic values that make its experience pertinent to them.

A major impetus to reform, as Rosovsky noted in the game, was that Harvard College had failed to examine the curricular consequences of the social, intellectual, and institutional changes in the academic world since World War II. Growth in the quantity, diversity, and importance of knowledge; the rise of professionalism; the multiplication of university functions; the heterogeneity of the student population—all of these led to a fragmentation of academic life. As a result the faculty's collegial mission, to furnish an undergraduate education, suffered a striking loss of structure and articulation. Charles Eliot's ideas about the character and goals of undergraduate education had been clear enough. He inherited a uniform and required curriculum designed to transmit to a social elite the "classical" learning that marked the educated gentleman. But Eliot saw the college's mission as preparing an intellectual elite for productive roles in society. To this end he set out to recruit an aristocracy of talent and to match its interests with a rich array of academic opportunities. The purpose of his elective system was to free both faculty and students from the restrictions of a narrowly defined intellectual culture, thus enabling them to invest their talents effectively in the study of congenial subjects. For undergraduates the point was not to acquire professional expertise, but rather through concentrated work to develop broadly applicable intellectual skills and qualities of mind that would serve them and society in later life.

Eliot's successors found important flaws in his conception of undergraduate education. Eliot assumed that the best and brightest students would have had a broad exposure to the various fields of knowledge and would thus to able to judge where their interests lay. But experience showed that often this was not the case. He also assumed a high degree of self-discipline and maturity among students, which proved to be at least an arguable notion. In any case, his successors concluded that the elective system was too radical a break with the past. Not only did it fail to foster intellectual seriousness and high levels of attainment, it also worked against the traditional belief that an educated person was one with a share in a common fund of knowledge and values.

Lowell's reforms modified Eliot's conception in several ways. They *required* students to invest part of their time in the concentrated study of a particular subject, and they provided a carrot and a stick for higher standards of achievement by introducing degree honors and a comprehensive examination. In addition, Lowell sought to counteract Eliot's insistence on individual differences by imposing distribution requirements on all students and by developing residential colleges to instill common values and standards of conduct.

The idea that undergraduate education should foster intellectual and social community lost ground steadily as the twentieth century wore on, despite the occasional successes of the general education movement. While not denying the powerful centrifugal forces in social and intellectual life, the leaders of that movement stressed the need for some common and binding learning capable of providing an effective counterforce. But the post-World War II transformation of higher education strained to the breaking point the belief in a shared fund of knowledge and values. If neither Eliot's nor Lowell's nor Conant's ideal sufficed, what, then, were the purposes of undergraduate education? To the Harvard faculty in the 1970s the answer seemed to lie in an educational standard compatible with the current realities of academic life and a practical-minded appraisal of students, of faculty, of the disciplines.

The social mission of the college already had been redefined by the admissions policies developed in the 1950s and 1960s. Harvard was free to select an intellectual elite well prepared at the country's leading secondary schools, but it decided to broaden its selection criteria to include not only academic ability but other qualities and characteristics as well. By the late 1960s the effort to recruit a national student body diverse in talents, background, personalities, and career goals was supremely successful. To be sure, most of Harvard students continued to come from professional and managerial families. But the initial idea of a "balanced class," in which preferments were justified on the basis of such factors as motivation, geographical residence, athletic or musical ability, and alumni connections, was increasingly influenced by ever-widening conceptions of social fairness.[4] Eventually it evolved into a Noah's Ark principle calling for the selection of the most academically fit exemplars of almost every variety of eighteen-year-old.

This was, of course, a far cry from Charles Eliot's conception of an aristocracy of talent. He had accepted heterogeneity of background as an incidental consequence of recruiting the best and brightest students. While the principle that academic ability must be the main standard of selection continued to have weight, heterogeneity now became an end in itself. The underlying aim of the new admissions policy was to assemble "a whole civilization"—a socially and culturally mixed group to which each member made some special contribution. The rationale was a widely shared belief that diversity would widen students' experience, enable them to learn from each other and, more particularly, learn to live with each other. The idea turned Lowell's notion of residential communities inside out. It was stripped of any intention to transform a diverse student population into a homogeneous educated class. Rather, admissions policy and college life alike were to set a standard of respect for the widest possible range of individual differences. Thus Harvard responded to the public demand for broader access to higher education by redefining the older ideal of community in terms of the new creed of social inclusiveness.

By the 1970s the commitment to a representative student body sometimes led, perversely, to an obsession with social group distinctions. The principles of equal educational opportunity and meritocratic recruitment had come to be tempered by the goal of a "critical mass" of racial and ethnic groups, in turn balanced by sex, socioeconomic status, and geographical background. Far from reducing social distances, the creation of these mini whole communities often tended to limit interaction, to foster a new ghettoization of student life and learning.

But the commitment to social diversity also explicitly acknowledged important features of the American educational system. In contrast to other democratic nations, there was in the United States no nationally standardized curriculum or systematic weeding out of the less successful performers at various stages of schooling. The American system is deliberately fluid and amorphous. It is designed for a mass market, and with notable exceptions, both public and private, its secondary schools do not devote themselves to the identification and development of an academic elite. Because the quality of secondary schooling varies enormously, selective liberal arts colleges cannot hope to reconcile their interest in social diversity with a high standard of academic preparation.

However, the primary purpose of these colleges is to foster intellectual achievement and discipline. Their problem—their dilemma—is to come up with a baseline for their students that both sets a goal for the less well prepared and is challenging to the better-prepared. Given the absence of a guiding standard, the practical consequence is that colleges merely provide, through the curriculum, the opportunity for students to find, or lose, their own way. Yet without such a standard, it is difficult to justify the admission of unevenly prepared students or to relate the educational program of the colleges to larger intellectual or social goals.

The problem was compounded by the luxuriant growth of

the college curriculum through the postwar period, when a place was found, particularly in university colleges, for almost every subject under the sun. This proliferation did not serve the needs of the average undergraduate. Instead it catered to those pursuing advanced work or "nontraditional" interests. The rising number of undergraduate concentrations, which spread beyond the confines of traditional departments, required no further justification in an academic culture that asserted the importance of knowing one subject well. But there was no credible mechanism or organizing principle to relate the growing range of knowledge to the intellectual development of undergraduates. Distribution requirements served only the negative purpose of preventing overspecialization, and on the whole they served it badly. Older ideals of a common learning made little sense to a faculty that shared no common corpus of knowledge valued or books read. Nor could anyone sustain conviction in an integrated set of ideas characterizing the natural sciences, the social sciences, or the humanities. Far from constituting a holy trinity of knowledge, these divisions came to be merely a *ménage à trois*.

Not surprisingly, the faculty looked to its own distinctive character for a solution. What was needed was a standard that related the work of scholars to the intellectual needs of most students. The faculty was not a group of educated men and women who had all read Plato or swam easily in the mainstream of Western thought and institutions. Nor was it divided into three parts, each of which shared common assumptions, approaches, and knowledge. Rather, it was a collection of scholars whose highly developed skills and analytic training were derived from traditional disciplines and were dedicated to the pursuit of knowledge for its own sake. What such a faculty could usefully teach to all undergraduates was how to go about addressing different kinds of problems and what skills they would need to do so.

It was both logical and inevitable that the intellectual problem of reformulating undergraduate general education resolved itself in the designation of a Core of ways of thinking and knowing framed by the traditional disciplines. This was a formulation that united the faculty's research and undergraduate teaching functions. The Core program did not follow the traditional distinction between general and specialized education, for many of its courses concentrated on narrowly defined topics or problems. Its crucial element was to increase students' intellectual versatility, not their specialized knowledge. The general education movement had battled resolutely against the breakdown of a common social and intellectual culture. The new curricular design of Harvard College made its peace with changing circumstance by living with—indeed, by trying to use—diversity, liberty, flexibility, and specialization.

It remains to be seen, of course, whether the new intellectual standard is as compatible in practice as it is in principle with the social values of Harvard's admissions policy. The issue will likely come to a head first over the science requirement. If, as a number of scientists and mathematicians predict, a "serious" science requirement cannot be effectively imposed on every student in Harvard College, what will give way—the science requirement or admissions criteria?

The Harvard experience illuminated one more feature of the academic landscape at the end of the 1970s. While there remains more than a trace of querulousness and cleavage, much of it fueled by declining financial resources, there is also a new and growing interest in finding practical solutions to internal problems. Few academics have failed to notice that the era of university expansion is over. The favorite incantation of budget officers, "more of this means less of that," echoes in the furthest corridors of academia. In addition, the reduced demand for college teachers—and, inevitably, for graduate training programs—has encouraged a reordering of academic priorities. At no time in the postwar history of higher education has there been a greater recognition of institutional limitations and of the need to strike a fresh balance among the university's scholarly, educational, and social missions. In contrast to the 1960s, the academic mood of the 1970s—and of the Core Curriculum that was its product—was inward-looking, preoccupied with academic values, prepared to trade off some modest degree of liberty for the sake of some modest sense of form and order, and driven by a practical desire to make the system work.

Appendix. A partial listing of Core courses, including only those offered in 1981-82.

Literature and Arts

Literature and Arts (A) Literature

Note: These courses aim at conveying an understanding of particular literary modes of apprehending and articulating experience.

Literature and Arts A-11. Theatre and Drama

A study of the specific nature of dramatic form. Readings include examples from periods of extreme formal development, selected for their provocative nature and the challenges they pose to traditional notions of dramatic expression. Will consider (among others) the Greek stage, Oriental dance drama, French neoclassicism, commedia dell'arte low farce, expressionism and poetic drama, and contemporary avant-garde tendencies.

Literature and Arts A-12. Great Novels of 19th and Early 20th Centuries

A close study of some major works from the great age of the novel, with attention to changing techniques of narration and characterization, the modes of fictional realism, and the development of the genre. The novelists to be considered in 1981-82 will include Jane Austen, Dickens, Stendhal, George Eliot, Flaubert, Hardy, Conrad, Lawrence, Joyce, and Virginia Woolf. Several films, adapted from prescribed novels, will be shown in conjunction with the course to illustrate parallels and differences between fictional and cinematic intentions.

Literature and Arts A-13. Chivalric Romances of the Middle Ages

A study of the genre of chivalric romance, with some attention to the use of chivalric themes and materials in later literature. Among the works to be studied are the romances of Chrétien de Troyes, Wolfram von Eschenbach's *Parsifal, Sir Gawain and the Green Knight,* Sir Thomas Malory's *Morte D'arthur,* and Cervantes' *Don Quixote.* All readings are in translation.

Literature and Arts A-15. Comedy and the Novel

An introduction to problems of comedy, of narrative, and of their interrelation as seen in the European tradition that begins with *Don Quixote.* Additional readings will include works by Fielding, Voltaire, Diderot, Byron, Gogol, Stendhal, and Bulgakov.

Literature and Arts A-19. Fiction, Ideology, and Myth: the Novel in the Twentieth Century

An examination of the novel and its cultural presuppositions and uses between 1900 and 1960. The emphasis will be on several related matters: on formal experiment and prose artistry, on the criticism of contemporary life and thought, and on imaginative literature as a distinct mode of knowledge, as realistic as science and as symbolic, and prophetic, as religion. Assigned readings will include British, American, and European novelists, particularly those who address themselves to modern ideological issues. Certain works of speculative argument will also be introduced into discussion.

Literature and Arts A-20. The Literature of Christian Reflection

An examination of certain classic and modern texts dealing with the Christian search for and experience of personal religious faith. Lectures will emphasize style, form, and the implications of the works for the lives of their authors. The approach will be primarily literary, interior, and biographical rather then theological or historical. The lives and works of modern authors will be compared with those of earlier periods. Authors to be studied will include Augustine, Juliana of Norwich, Teresa of Avila, Luther, Calvin, Donne, Hopkins, Kierkegaard, Weil, O'Connor, and Bonhoffer.

Literature and Arts A-21. The Literary Mind of the Middle Ages

The wide-spread assumption of the compactness of the Medieval mind will be scrutinized and corrected through the reading of different authors and the identification of diversified Medieval trends in literature. The literature of the self from St. Augustine's *Confessions* to Petrarch's *Secretum* will be explored as well as the complex attitude of the Medieval authors toward the classical past. The Medieval view of art will be studied taking also into account its most relevant philosophical background from Boethius to St. Thomas Aquinas' part of the *Summa* dealing with human passions. Readings from English as well as from Latin, Provençal, French, and Italian texts in English translation (lyric, epic, narrative, and dramatic poetry will be included). The techniques of long poems from *Roland's lied* to Dante's *Divine Comedy* will be carefully analyzed.

Literature and Arts A-22. Poets, Poems, and Poetry

A study of poetry as the history and science of feeling: readings in major lyric poems of England and America. Emphasis on problems of invention and execution, and on poet's choice of genre, stance, context, and structure. Other topics to be raised include the process of composition, the situating of a poem in a volume and in its historical and poetic contexts, the notion of a poet's development, the lyric as dramatic speech, and the experimental lyric of the twentieth century.

Literature and Arts A-23. Realistic Novel and Social Consciousness in Nineteenth Century France

Realistic novels are fictional tales representing not only the actions and reactions of individual characters, but also, in considerable detail, the social structures with which these individuals interact in decisive phases of their progress. This important literary form, developed in the 19th century, has had an impact that reaches beyond the esthetic or artistic domain of literature: by its careful representation of social and psychological conditions, it has broadened the social consciousness of its readers and given them a more articulate perception of the world. The course will illustrate this function in connection with a study of major texts by the great French masters: Stendhal, Balzac, Flaubert, Zola, and Maupassant.

Literature and Arts A-24. The Contemporary Latin American Novel

An examination of some of the major questions confronting Latin America as formulated by the novels of its most representative authors. Works will be placed in their national and cultural contexts, but special attention will be given to narrative devices and literary techniques underlying their themes. Readings will include novels by Carpentier, Asturias, Onetti, Cortázar, Rulfo, García, Márquez, Fuentes, and Vargas Llosa.

Note: All works will be read in English or Spanish.

Literature and Arts (B) Fine Arts and Music

Note: These courses incorporate instruction in the elements of visual or aural "literacy" through direct exposure to the works of major artists.

Literature and Arts B-16. Abstraction in Modern Art

A critical examination of the theory and practice of so-called abstract art in the 20th century, with particular attention paid to the apparent need of such art for elaborate legitimations, explanations, ontological excuses. Are we right to lump together under the rubric 'abstraction' anti-figurative revolutionary propaganda (Lissitsky), sophisticated primitivism (Pollock), or cod-mysticism (Mondrian)? Due weight will be given to the enemies and critics of abstraction, but also to the countering question: if abstract art in our time has proved, on the whole, regressive and reductive, is not the same true–perhaps truer still–of the figurative art done in opposition to it? Discussion sections will concentrate on texts: Schapiro, Greenberg, Gombrich, Art-Language.

*Literature and Arts B-17. The Studio Arts, Theoretical and Practical Explorations

An exploration of drawing painting, and sculpture through lectures and studio projects with a focus on current practice.

Literature and Arts B-18. Design and the Environmental Arts, Theoretical and Practical Explorations

An exploration of the designed environment through lectures and studio projects. Begins with the investigation of basic materials and techniques and concludes with the design of habitat and urban form.

Literature and Arts B-22. Ancient and Classical Painting

An introduction to drawing and painting; a study of Greek and Roman painting, as a self-contained tradition creating itself, and as a series of classical experiments in forming three-dimensional illusions on flat surfaces. Line, contour, space, depth, volume, foreshortening, perspective, color, shadow and highlight, and style will be emphasized, and observed in drawing and painting on wood, clay, plaster, and stone, with techniques of engraving, pen, brush, encaustic, and mosaic. Classical modes of handling human and animal figures, historical and mythological narrative, expressions of feeling and drama, portraiture and landscape. Classical solutions to general artistic challenges will be set off against other systems in Egyptian, Aegean, Near Eastern and Etruscan painting, and will be related to philosophical, scientific, literary, and historical developments.

Literature and Arts B-23. Monuments of Japan

Devoted to a small number of major architectural monuments which demonstrate Japanese criteria of beauty and modes of visual expression. Lectures and reading will analyze basic systems of construction, and the relationship of buildings to the landscape and garden settings; considerable attention will be given to individual works of art normally associated with the structures, and with the identity of the patrons, their social and cultural aspirations. Monuments will include the Ise Grand Shrine, Buddhist sanctuaries such as Todai-ji and Daitoku-ji, the Katsura Villa, and the Nijo Castle. Sections will provide opportunity to examine at first hand original works of art in collections in Harvard and the greater Boston are.

Literature and Arts B-51. The Literature of the Voice

The focus will be on several significant works from each genre. The genres will include motet, mass, cantata, anthem, madrigal, and chanson; and the examples will range from medieval to current. Whenever possible, the class will perform the pieces discussed.

Literature and Arts B-54. The Development of the String Quartet

An investigation of selected quartets which will provide a basis for comparison of the compositional processes of Haydn, Mozart, Beethoven, Shubert, Mendelssohn, Brahms, Debussy, and Ravel. The study will focus on differences of sound and style.

Literature and Arts B-55. Opera: Perspectives on Music and Drama

An introduction to opera as an art-form, exploring some of the ways in which it conveys dramatic action through musical form and expression. Examples will be drawn chiefly but not exclusively from works by Mozart, Verdi, and Wagner.

Literature and Arts B-56. Structure and Form through Music and Movement

A study of traditional forms in music using representative works from the 17th to the 19th centuries. The objective is to develop aural and visual awareness through analysis and direct application. Illustration and analysis of the elements of sound and movement (melody, harmony, rhythm, texture, and phraseology) will include prototypes which will be developed as a glossary of terms used in the course. These terms will serve as tools for the analysis of the forms covered in the lectures. Movement will be used to elucidate the relationships of these elements within the form or, in the words of D.H. Prall, to elucidate "Content being formed." Will utilize team teaching and will communicate to the musician's ear through the dancer's eye and to the dancer's eye through the musician's ear.

Literature and Arts (C) Contexts of Culture

Note: These courses illustrate the connection among the arts or with prevailing ideas and concepts, and place artistic achievements in their social or intellectual contexts.

Literature and Arts C-14. The Concept of the Hero in Hellenic Civilization

Alternative perspectives on the individual and society. An intensive study of the archaic Greek hero in literature, art, and cult. Selected readings, in translation, of Homer, Hesiod, Herodotus, the poets of lyric and tragedy.

Note: Meets the Core requirement in Foreign Cultures.

Literature and Arts C-17. The Sublime in America

The search for an American aesthetic in literature and the visual arts in the early national and Romantic periods, tracing the process of Americanization of ideas of the sublime, the beautiful, and the picturesque, and their implications for American character, landscape, and destiny. Writers include Irving, Cooper, Emerson, Thoreau, Hawthorne, Whitman and Melville; painters include West, Allston, Cole, Church, Bierstadt and the luminists.

Literature and Arts C-19. Renaissance Images of Man

An examination of various concepts of man, his nature, his potentialities and limits, and his role in society as expressed and illustrated in selected masterpieces of literature, philosophy, painting, sculpture, and architecture from c. 1300–1650.

Literature and Arts C-20. The Function and Criticism of Literature

The major approaches to literature and the arts as a whole from classical antiquity to the present, and the theory of literature and art generally. Emphasis will be given to the moral and educational values in literature and the humanities. Concepts and approaches stressed will be Classicism, the Renaissance and Neo-Classicism, Romanticism, Realism and Naturalism, and the rise of Modernism. Readings will be in the major critics from Aristotle and the Greeks to the 20th century.

Literature and Arts C-21. The Enlightenment and the Transition to Romanticism

The period that transforms our Renaissance legacy into modern values; topics in literature, the arts, and thought generally from 1700–1820, especially the creation (1750 on) of a modern world-view. The great shift from Classic to Romantic in all the arts. Rationalism as it enters an age of feeling and then creates–and partially resists–the Romantic Era. New views of nature and human nature; individualism–Locke, Shaftesbury, Voltaire, Rousseau, Wordsworth. Revolutions social and industrial–Burke, Jefferson. Gibbon and the rise of history. Kant; why transcendentalism developed. The novel, the idea of the imagination and the flowering of Romantic poetry–Keats and Coleridge. Other figures include Pope, Goethe, Johnson, Franklin, Mozart, Beethoven.

Literature and Arts C-23. Art and Politics in Europe 1700–1871

Examines the interaction of art and politics during a period of change and upheaval in European culture. It is less a formal study of changes in artistic styles than an examination of the theme of "engagement" by artists in the events of their time. It is also concerned with the political uses of art and architecture in the service of ideologies, and with the social forms–academies; monuments; popular "festivals"; competitions, etc.–in which this propaganda was expressed. Students will be expected to master the outline of the political history of this period as well as acquiring a grasp of the simpler techniques of art history appropriate for this time.

Literature and Arts C-24. Paris and London in the Nineteenth Century

Comparative treatment of these two world cities in terms of the growth and development of an urban culture. The course will focus on the ways in which people experienced life in these cities and on the significance of the urban environment for those poets, novelists, architects, painters, illustrators, and photographers who helped to create a powerful image of the modern city.

Literature and Arts C-25. Drama and Theater in Medieval Society

Examines seven master works of medieval theater and the manner in which they (and some others) were staged in churches and towns from the perspective of conditions peculiar to time and place: drama as religious worship, in service to politics, as part of emerging city culture, as civic ostentation and religious duty, as reaction to the Reformation. In addition: the role of music in medieval plays, religious art in its influence on costumes, properties, and acting style, the architectural setting. Towns and regions studied: Fleury (The Herod Play), Beauvais (Daniel), 12th century Bavaria (the Antichrist), Arras (Bodel's Miracle Play of St. Nicholas, Adam de la Halle's "Bower" Comedy), Wakefield and York (the Corpus Christi Pageants), Lucerne (Passion Play, 1583). Several illustrated lectures, videotape of the York pageants.

Literature and Arts C-26. The Burden of the Past and the Greek Poet

"The Burden of the Past" is probably the main cultural challenge which nations on the site of ancient çivilizations have had to face in modern times. This course concentrates on the response of the Greeks to the challenge in the 20th century, with particular attention to poets, who were naturally among its most eloquent champions and interpreters. Emphasis is given to Palamas, Sikelianos, Cavafy, Seferis, Ritsos, and Elytis. Selected passages will be examined, with reference to comtemporary art and architecture, as well as to the social and political background of Greece in the first half of the 20th century.

Literature and Arts C-27. Renaissance Rome: Society, the Arts, and Religion in the Sixteenth Century

The study of the Papal capital at its peak focuses on three generations: *The Classical Period* of consolidation of power reflected in the social structure, art and urbanism of the High Renaissance; the *Response to International Tensions*–Protestant Reformation, the Sack of Rome, Catholic Reform, Mannerist Art; *The Counter Reformation*: the response of the Church, the new urban plan of Sixtus V, the religious art of Michelangelo's last years and the new art of the end of the century. The aim of the course is to show by a synchronic approach how the diverse ways in which a distinctive society expresses itself are structurally interrelated.

Note: Section leaders from different disciplines will emphasize a particular theme in which they are expert.

Literature and Arts C-28. Politics, Mythology, and Art in Bronze Age China

The Bronze Age (c. 2000–500 B.C.) of China was a period of fierce political contention among states and among kin groups, and it was also a period in which great works of art were produced. In this course we seek to examine how the Chinese Bronze Age arts–both the art of the written word and the visual arts–may be understood and appreciated in their political context. The course also serves to demonstrate some of the advantages of an interdisciplinary approach to ancient art and literature. Students will first be introduced to the Bronze Age civilization of China through acquaintence with the major literary texts (in translation), the contemporary documents (mainly bronze and oracle bone inscriptions), and the results of archaeological research.

Literature and Arts C-29. The Heroic Tradition in Northern Europe

The concept of the hero in the literature, mythology, and culture of the late Viking period and after, relating Old Norse epic traditions to those of England and Germany. The course surveys the development of the hero in Germanic tradition from the earliest poems to the courtly romance, focusing on the interplay between changing cultural institutions such as the transition from paganism to Christianity, the growth of national kingdoms from local chiefdoms and the colonization of Iceland and Greenland, and the presentation of the hero in literature and art. Readings include the Poetic and Prose *Eddas*, several Norse sagas, *Beowulf*, *Das Nibelungenlied*, and other shorter works.

Literature and Arts C-30. The French Renaissance

Concentrates on the reigns of Francis I and Henri II. This brilliant period played a decisive role in defining the character of French culture and produced works that still affect us deeply. The emphasis will be on the fine arts, especially the royal chateaux (Chambord, Fontainebleau, the Louvre). All the arts will be considered as they contributed to make a decor for social life. The major ideas and changing values of the time will also be examined in the literature (Rabelais, Ronsard, and the Pleiade, Montaigne).

Historical Study

Historical Study (A)

Note: These broad ranging courses explain historically the background and development of major aspects of the modern world, global or near global in dimension. They help the student understand, through historical study, some of the great issues–often problematic, policy issues–of our own world, and to experience history as an approach to understanding contemporary problems.

Historical Study A-11. Development and Underdevelopment: The Historical Origins of the Inequality of Nations

The subject is the marked divergence of Europe and its overseas offshoots from the rest of the world–in technology, economic and social organization, income and wealth, values and patterns of behavior. Going back to the Middle Ages, when Europe changed over from a state of compression to one of expansion, the course considers the implications of this disparity for the condition of other nations and peoples; examines the determinants and experience of imitation and emulation; and uses the historical record to throw light on the problems of economic development and inequality.

Historical Study A-12. International Conflicts in the Modern World

A discussion of three kinds of interstate conflicts: (a) those resulting from the rise and competing claims of nationalisms, (b) those stemming from clashes of ideological systems, and (c) those bred by economic exploitation and inequality.

The first half of the course will examine the 19th century antecedents of 20th century conflicts (the effect of nationalism on the European balance of power and the scramble for colonies), and the origins and consequences of the two World Wars. The second half will focus on the main international conflicts since 1945 (the Cold War, the problem of nuclear weapons, decolonization, regional conflicts, and the problem of creating a new international economic order) and attempts to control or solve them.

Historical Study A-13. Tradition and Transformation in East Asian Civilization: China

Modern China presents a dual image: a society transforming itself through economic development and social revolution; and the world's largest and oldest bureaucratic state, coping with longstanding problems of economic and political management. It is now recognized that whatever form of modern society and state emerges in China will bear the indelible imprint of China's historical experience, of her patterns of philosophy and religion, and of her social and political thought. These themes will be discussed, both as preludes to an understanding of China in the modern world, and as fundamentals of a great world civilization that developed along lines radically different from our own. The analysis will be implicitly comparative at every point, as we draw conceptual relationships between China's thought and institutions, and those we are familiar with in the West.
Note: Meets the Core Requirement in Foreign Cultures.

Historical Study A-14. Tradition and Transformation in East Asian Civilization: Japan

The most striking modern transformation in the world is that of Japan during the past century. Today it is economically powerful, culturally rich, politically democratic, and socially free and stable, ranking in all these respects among the world leaders. This course will inquire into the roots of Japanese civilization, studying its history, traditional institutions, society, religious and intellectual development, and aesthetic achievements, before examining comparatively and in more detail the process by which Japan has transformed itself into the nation it is today.
Note: Meets the Core requirement in Foreign Cultures.

Historical Study A-19. Nationalism, Religion, and Politics in Central Eurasia

Traces the changes in conceptions of ethnic identity and the related changes in the bases of political action among the peoples of Central Eurasia, a region defined as comprising Turkey, Iran, the Crimean and Kazan Tatar areas, Soviet Central Asia and Kazakhstan, Afghanistan, Pakistan, Kashmir, Chinese Inner Asia (Inner Mongolia, Sinkiang, and Tibet), and the Mongolian People's Republic. Emphasis on the 19th and 20th centuries.

Note: Meets the Core requirement in Foreign Cultures.

Historical Study A-22. **The Emergence of Women as a Force in Modern Society: The American Experience**

Examines the role of women in the development of American society from the mid-nineteenth century to the present as one continuous historical process. Analyzes the origins of the woman's movement and responses it evoked, focusing on issues of contemporary concern including education, economics, politics, religion, health, and family relations. Highlights differences in the experiences of women as individuals and as members of various socioeconomic, ethnic, racial, and regional groups. Contrasts historical patterns in the lives of men and women. Provides a historical background for understanding issues raised by the current wave of feminist activism.

Historical Study A-24. Historical Development of the International Political Economy

Explores the connections between politics and economic issues in Western societies since the seventeenth century. Topics include mercantilist, liberal, and protectionist theories of development; the emergence of imperialism and tariffs; international monetary systems from the gold standard to Bretton Woods; interwar inflation and mass unemployment; U.S. economic ascendancy from World War II to the 'stagflation' of the 1970's. Some background in elementary economics is desirable.

Historical Study (B)

Note: These sharply focused courses examine in detail the complexity of controversial and transforming events in the past which do not bear directly on contemporary policy questions. They involve close analysis of specific circumstances, motives, and decisions. The aim is to develop an understanding of the intricacy of the historical process: the way in which a variety of forces–economic, cultural, political–have interacted with individual aspirations and decisions to shape some significant portion of the world.

Historical Study B-10. The World of the Early Christians

Examines the ferment and cross-currents within Judaism and the Jewish conflict with Hellenism and Rome during the two centuries before the Christian era as a background to the emergence of the Christian movement, which is seen as a continuation of these developments. Traces the confrontation of Christianity with the pagan world of the Roman Empire, especially in the Greek east, with emphasis on the forms of literature and thought which were available to convey the Christian message and which helped at the same time to transform a Jewish sect into a gentile religion.

Historical Study B-16. The Scientific Revolution

The revolution that produced modern science considered from a critical and historical point of view, in its intellectual and social setting. The history and analysis of the concept of revolution. The scientific revolution compared with other kinds of revolutions in thought and action. The permanent influence of the scientific revolution. Some central topics to be discussed: experiment and observation vs. mathematics in the scientific revolution; magic and Hermeticism in relation to the new science; Protestantism and the rise of science in the 17th century; social or economic factors in the scientific revolution; philosophical background of the new science and the "experimental method;" science and religious belief; science and technology. A study will be made of the institutionalization of science: the organization of scientists into scientific societies and academies, the first communications revolution, science and the state. Readings will be assigned from the writings of the major scientists who created the scientific revolution, and from recent and present-day philosophers, historians, scientists, and sociologists.

Note: There are no scientific prerequisites. Discussion sections are designed to permit in-depth pursuit of one aspect of the main subject. If possible, there will be special sections for students with advanced scientific preparation.

Historical Study B-26. The Great Rebellion: Britain 1640–1660

Examines both the social and economic circumstances and the course of events from the meeting of the Long Parliament to the restoration of Charles II and also the principal themes of political and social thought during the period in an effort to comprehend the causes, character, and the consequences of the upheaval. Authors included are the Leveller pamphleteers, Winstanley, Hobbes, Milton, and Harrington.

Historical Study B-31. The Revolutionary Transformation of America

The origins and development of the American Revolution; the struggle over political principles and the relation of these principles to the social order; war and social readjustment; the emergence of basic doctrines of American political belief and the effort to embody these doctrines in public institutions; the transformation of American society, politics, and government in the Revolutionary era. Emphasis on the relation of politics and political ideas to social development.

Historical Study B-46. The Darwinian Revolution

An examination of the intellectual structure and social context of evolutionary theory as it developed in the 19th and early 20th centuries. Topics include the backgrounds to various forms of evolutionary thought; Darwin's methodology; the relations between biological and social evolutionary thought; the comparative reception of Darwinian evolutionary theory in Great Britain, France, Germany, and the U.S.; and the Darwinian Revolution as a scientific revolution.

Historical Study B-56. The Russian Revolution

Russia from 1900 to 1921. The course will trace, in part analytically, in part by means of a narrative, the gradual dissolution of the Imperial Regime, the chaos of 1917, and the creation of a new state under Lenin's dictatorship. Heavy stress will be laid on the aspirations and actions of the peasantry, the intelligentsia, and bureaucratic-police establishment, the three protagonists of the Russian Revolution.

Social Analysis

These courses are designed to familiarize students with some of the central approaches explaining human behavior in contemporary society. They are not, in most cases, intended to serve as an introduction to, or a survey of, a social science concentration. In general, the courses are organized around a significant problem or theme that can be analyzed by the use of formal theories tested with empirical data.

Social Analysis 10 (formerly Economics 10). Principles of Economics

Survey of microeconomics, macroeconomics and the principal applied areas of the discipline. The course examines the historical origins of economics, the underlying assumptions, and the principal critiques. Models explore individual and group behavior in the market, as well as current policy issues such as antitrust and regulation, income distribution, inflation, trade barriers, and economic development.

Note: The course is taught in sections with occasional lectures. Students may select among different types of sections based on their needs and interests. The course is designed for both students planning no further work in the field as well as potential concentrators.

Social Analysis 11. Conceptions of Human Nature

Examines certain important ideas about human nature. Emphasis is given to the works of Marx, Freud, Maslow, Skinner and psychological empiricism. Each approach will be considered in terms of its philosophical basis, its support from systematic data sources, and–most particularly–its effect upon social and political decisions in the real world. While the main focus will be from the standpoint of psychology, we shall also be concerned with the contributions of philosophy and history to these questions.

Social Analysis 18. Culture and Human Development

A description of the universal psychological qualities that characterize human development from infancy to adolescence and a consideration of how the structure, beliefs, and practices of a particular society influence the time course of developmental competences, the relationship of the growing child to the family and the profile of values, motives and skills acquired during childhood.

Social Analysis 19. Explaining the Holocaust and the Phenomenon of Genocide

Drawing on the resources of sociology and psychology this course will seek to explain the attempts at exterminating whole human groups. The following themes will be discussed: sources of aggression, scapegoating, varieties of racism, justifications for mass murders, the mentality of the executioners, social behavior in catastrophic circumstances, life in ghettos and concentration camps. The course will study the Jewish Holocaust, the massacre of the Armenians, the slaughter in Cambodia, and other genocides of the recent and distant past.

Social Analysis 20. The Clash of Cultures: Conflict, Cooperation, and Change in the Ancient and Modern Worlds

What happens when two very different cultures encounter one another? Are warfare and conquest the inevitable results, or are peaceful interchanges possible? This course examines the topic of contact and acculturation from anthropological and historical perspectives and attempts to reach general conclusions about the changes produced by the clash of cultures. Specific case studies include Greek and Roman interaction with the "barbarian" cultures of Europe, interchanges between Indians and Europeans through the North American fur trade, the British colonization of Australia, the Spanish conquest of Peru, and contacts between Vikings and Eskimos in Greenland.

Moral Reasoning

These courses focus on the investigation of significant and recurrent questions of choice and value that arise in ordinary moral and political experience. Though they will not be chiefly concerned with the history of philosophy, the courses will draw on the major writings of moral and political philosophers to illuminate the intricacies of ethical argument on such matters as justice, law, democracy, obligation, and citizenship.

Moral Reasoning 11. Types of Ethical Theory

A critical analysis of the principle ethical theories and their practical application to problems concerning the individual and society. Among the topics considered are skepticism, relativism, egoism, hedonism, utilitarianism, justice, punishment, and freedom. Readings are from contemporary sources, and from the works of the great philosophers, both ancient and modern.

Moral Reasoning 15.   Democratic Theory and its Critics

Examines the basic theory of democratic government as well as the central arguments urged for and against the reasonableness and even the possibility of democracy. Readings include Rousseau, Paine, Burke, Jefferson, Madison, Tocqueville, Mill, Mosca, Michels, and Schumpeter.

Moral Reasoning 21.   The Philosophy of Law

Introduction to legal philosophy examining the degree and sense in which the decision of cases at law depend on moral and political analysis. Will begin by studying a number of case reports in different areas of law, then consider, against the background of these cases, leading theories about the concept of law and standards for adjudication, including positivism, the theory of economic analysis, and the rights thesis. Will then consider a number of recent controversial decisions by the Supreme Court, particularly in the application of the equal protection clause of the United States Constitution, together with materials in political and moral philosophy that treat the substantive political issues raised in these cases.

Moral Reasoning 22.   Justice

A critical analysis of selected classical and contemporary theories of justice, with discussion of present-day practical applications, such as: quotas and reverse discrimination, civil disobedience, military conscription, income distribution, meritocracy, equality of opportunity versus equality of result. Readings to include Aristotle, Locke, Mill, Kant, Marx, and Rawls.

Science

Science (A)

Note: These courses are intended to introduce students to areas of science dealing primarily with deductive and quantitative aspects and to increase the student's understanding of the physical world.

Science A-15.   Dynamics and Energy: Concepts and Applications

Presents physics as a body of knowledge and process of investigation, with reference to its historical development and relationship to modern technology. Topics include: Motion, its description and causes; Newtonian celestial mechanics; the Scientific and Industrial Revolutions; development of the Theory of Heat, Energy, and Thermodynamics; and a survey of the concepts underlying modern energy technology.   *Prerequisite:* High school mathematics through trigonometry. Some exposure to high school physics or chemistry is helpful, but not assumed.

Science A-16. Modern Physics: Concepts and Development

Presents physics as a body of knowledge and a process of investigation, with emphasis on recent achievements. Topics include: Special Relativity, Quantum Mechanics, Electromagnetism, Waves, and an introduction to Elementary Particles.

Note: Taken together, Science A-15 and A-16 provide an integrated year-long introduction to the basic concepts of physics. Either may be taken separately, and will satisfy the Core requirement in Science A.

Prerequisite: Science A-15 or one year of high school physics.

Science A-17. The Astronomical Perspective

Scientific discovery and our understanding of the cosmos. Fall term: Gravitation as the ruling force in the universe– from the planetary theories of the ancient Greeks to pulsars, black holes, and quasars in an Einsteinian cosmology. Will gravity cause an ultimate collapse of the universe? Spring term: Evolution as a central theme in science–the birth and death of stars, the origin of the elements, the formation of the solar system, and the emergence and evolution of life on Earth. Is there intelligent life elsewhere? These topics form the framework for an inquiry into the nature of science from the philosophical, historical, and ethical perspective of the astronomer.

Note: Taken as a full course meets the Core requirement in both Science A and Science B.

Science A-18. Space, Time and Motion

An inquiry into intuitive, philosophical, mathematical, and physical notions of space, time, and motion: how they have developed, how they are related, and how we can assess their validity. Intuitive and philosophical views of space and time in the light of modern biology and psychology; time and continuity; Newton's theory and its genesis: Einstein's theories of space, time, and gravitation; cosmology.

Note: Taken as a full course, Science A-18 meets the Core requirement in both Science A and Science B. Sections function as independent seminars with a common syllabus and common reading and writing assignments. Section assignments take account of previous knowledge of mathematics.

Science A-20. From Alchemy to Elementary Particle Physics

Chronicles the search for the most basic constituents of all matter, and for the rules by which they combine. Begins with the 19th-century vindication of early Greek notions of element and atom, and proceeds through a study of the basic laws of physics and how they have evolved. Recent exciting developments in elementary-particle physics are seen as natural continuations of past endeavors; how our present understanding of atomic and sub-atomic structure results from a complex interplay between experimental and theoretical research. The study of several key developments in historical perspective (the explanation of combustion, the observation of radioactivity, the theory of relativity, etc.) leads to an appreciation of the current research frontier.

Science A-24. Dynamics of the Earth

A way of studying the Earth emphasizing dynamics of large-scale physical and chemical processes. Topics covered: the nature of seismic waves and the structure of the solid planet; the geological-geochemical-petrological cycle; the chemistry of rock weathering and land surface processes; plate tectonics–mid-ocean ridges, transform faults, trenches and subduction zones, hot spots, mechanisms of plate motions, magnetic anomalies, polar wandering; origin of igneous, metamorphic and sedimentary rock types, structural deformation and mountain building; the origin of Earth and the overall history of the planet.

Prerequisite: Secondary school physics and chemistry and mathematics through trigonometry.

Science A-25. Chemistry of the 20th Century

The areas of chemistry are structure, reactions and applications. Structural topics are particles, nuclei, atoms, bonds, molecules, crystals, polymers (including biopolymers), and stereochemistry. Reactions include thermodynamics, inorganic and organic reactions, enzymes, and nucleic acids. Applications include the relationships of chemistry to life processes, energy, and the environment.

Science A-26. The World's Microstructure: Particles and Waves in Modern Physics

A survey of our present understanding of the way in which matter and light are made up of elementary particles. Central themes will include the wave-particle duality of modern quantum theory and its accompanying principles of uncertainty and complementarity. Applications of these principles to the structure of molecules, atoms, and nuclei are shown to explain the basis of a great deal of our physical experience. Many of the phenomena discussed are illustrated by lecture demonstrations, and several by experiments to be performed in laboratory sessions.

Prerequisite: Some competence in elementary algebra and geometry.

Science A-27. Sound and Hearing

An exploration of the physical, anatomical, physiological, and psychological mechanisms involved in human hearing. The term begins with an introduction to the physics of waves and oscillators, and proceeds with an examination of auditory phenomena. The aim of the course is to introduce nonscientists to the physical description of sound excitations, to describe their transduction by the ear into language of neural pulses in the central nervous system, to describe and illustrate the corresponding behavior manifestations including various important illusions, and to explore the interplay of physics and behavior involved in speech, music, sensory aids, high-fidelity sound, speech synthesis, and the like. Throughout, it is stressed that noise processes and other chance fluctuations impose limitations on the processes of information transfer and on our ability to make estimates and inferences from samples of data.

Science (B)

Note: These courses are intended to provide a general understanding of science as a way of looking at man and the world by introducing students to complex natural systems with a substantial historical or evolutionary component.

Science B-15. Evolutionary Biology

The first principles of evolutionary theory, genetics, classification, ecology, and behavior; a phylogenetic synopsis of the major groups of organisms from viruses to primates; comparative physiology with reference to environmental adaptation. A consideration of the origins of human social behavior and of the relation of biology to the social sciences and humanities.

Science B-16. History of the Earth and of Life

Major aspects of the physical and biological history of our earth (geology and paleontology). Part 1 (historical science) uses the historical development of theories about earth history to examine styles of doing science when faced with complex histories or unrepeated events. Also outlines the "big" questions that students of earth history have always asked– does time have a direction; does change have a characteristic tempo? Part 2 (physical history) develops the theory of plate tectonics and examines how far it can serve as a general model for interpreting the earth's physical history. Topics include: planetary geology, history of the earth-moon system, early development of continents, atmospheres and oceans, history of continental drift. Part 3 (biological history) begins with an examination of Darwinian theory and assesses its application as a general model for explaining the history of life. Topics include: origin of life, rapid extinctions and periods of origination as characteristic of life's history, vertebrate origins, dinosaurs, and human evolution.

Science B-22. Cellular Communication

An examination of how living cells communicate. The first section of the course discusses cell structure with special reference to communication and signaling within individual cells. Emphasis is placed on the management of genetic information and, more particularly, its derepression and flow from the genes in the nucleus to the synthetic centers in the cytoplasm. The second part of the course deals with communication between living cells by means of the nervous and endocrine systems and by neuroendocrine mechanisms. The final section considers the role of cellular communication in the development and integration of complex organisms.

Science B-23. The Human Organism

An introduction to physiological processes operating in human cells, organs, organ systems, and organisms as they respond to a changing environment. The course emphasizes how basic physical and chemical laws regulate the form and function of cells and organisms. Basic physiological concepts such as control, transport, and homeostasis will be presented as will general responses to infection, injury and trauma. The second half of the course discusses particular organ systems. This year the cardiovascular, pulmonary, and reproductive systems will be emphasized.

Science B-24. Classical and Molecular Genetics

The living world as seen from the perspective of genetics and evolution. Original works of major importance will be read and discussed as the course traces the principal discoveries of classical, molecular, and population genetics, and considers some of the main problems at the forefront of current thought and research.

Science B-25. Microbial and Molecular Biology

Surveys from a historical perspective, the emergence of bacteria as model cells, the development of bacterial genetics and of molecular biology, and the resulting coherent picture of cell organization and function. Topics include the nature and limits of the scientific method; molecular information storage and transfer as the unique attribute of living organisms; the mechanisms for preserving a genetic program, creating genetic novelty, translating one-dimensional genetic information into 3-dimensional proteins, catalyzing metabolic reactions, and assembling the products into cells; and the role of protein allostery in regulating the development of genetic potentialities and in mediating responses to the environment. The implications of this knowledge for evolutionary unity and diversity, for our understanding of man, and for selected philosophical and social problems will be briefly considered.

Prerequisite: Chemistry 5a or a high school course in chemistry.

Foreign Cultures

These courses expand the student's range of cultural experience by examining a major civilization and provide fresh perspectives on the student's own cultural assumptions and traditions.

Foreign Cultures 12. Sources of Indian Civilization

An introduction to the ideas and images which shaped classical Indian civilization and which continue to be of significance to the understanding of modern India. The course will explore three areas of Indian culture: its philosophical perspectives, its social and moral order, and its mythic and visual imagination.

Foreign Cultures 16. Introduction to Chinese Culture

Traditional Chinese philosophy, literature, art, and music. Selected major works are studied (in English translation) as representatives of each field and for what they tell us about Chinese artistic and cultural values generally. Topics include Confucian and Taoist thought, medieval poetry and landscape painting, Ming and Ch'ing dynasty novels, and musical narratives.

Foreign Cultures 17. Thought and Change in the Contemporary Middle East

Focus on Iran, Turkey, Egypt and North Africa, how both natives and non-native social theorists portray the processes of change and tradition. Orientalist, Marxist and cultural anthropological theorists will be juxtaposed; writers such as Gökalp, Shariati, Fanon will be situated. Topics will include Islam and politics; economic change; restricted literacy and culture; alienation identity and healing.

Foreign Cultures 18. Comparative Politics of Latin America

Focus on formation and development of political cleavages and cleavage systems and of mass-based political groups (parties, unions, peasant federations, ethnicity, religion, private foreign investment, industrialization) comparatively and through time in Spanish and Portuguese speaking countries in the Americas. Analysis of the expansion of mass political participation, elections, the impact of the military and military rule on political groups and cleavages, and the impact of international factors on these actors and issues.

Note: Meets the Core requirement in Foreign Cultures only for students in sections using the Spanish language.

Foreign Cultures 19. The Civilization of South American Indians

The history and culture of South American Indians, focusing particularly on the contrast between Andean civilization and the way of life of the lowland peoples. The differing styles and emphasis of these culture areas will be explored, as also the theories which have tried to account for them.

Foreign Cultures 20. Indo-Muslim Culture and the Arts

An introduction to the Islamic culture of Pakistan, India, and Bangladesh through an examination of the historical development of its dominant arts. Central topics include Mughal architecture and miniature painting; Persian and Urdu lyric poetry; classical music and dance; minor arts. Explores the relationship among these arts with reference to form and structure. Contextual considerations include relevant social, political, and religious phenomena.

Foreign Cultures 21. The Literature of the Spanish-speaking Peoples from 1898 to the Present

Covers eight decades of the literature of the Spanish- speaking peoples, from the Spanish-American War and its intellectual consequences to the present, with the Spanish Civil War (1936) as a dividing line. The first half centers on the Spanish Age of Unamuno and Garcia Lorca (1898–1936), while the second considers the contemporary flowering of Hispanic American fiction and poetry (Borges, Neruda, García Márquez). It emphasizes the dual role of literature, as reflection of a society and as maker of paradigms for that society. Particular attention is given to the cultural contrasts of the United States and Hispanic America as seen by authors such as Rodó and Octavio Paz.
Note: Conducted in Spanish.

Foreign Cultures 23. The Culture of Modern Germany: From the Empire to the Nazi Era

Literary texts and cultural documents from the period spanning 1890 to 1939. Discussion of works by Nietzsche, Toller, Brecht, Hesse, Kafka, Mann, and others.

Note: Designed for students who wish to develop a reading knowledge of German. Both Foreign Cultures 23 and 24 have to be taken to fulfill the Foreign Cultures requirement. *Prerequisite:* German A, German Bab, or equivalent preparation.

Foreign Cultures 24. Turn-of-the-Century Austrian Culture

Continuation of German 25 or German Ca. Literary texts and cultural documents from turn-of-the-century Austria. Authors include Schnitzler, Hofmannsthal, Freud, Musil, Zweig, and others.
                Prerequisite: German Ca, German Da, Foreign Cultures 23, or equivalent preparation.

Foreign Cultures 26. Industrial East Asia

Examines the variant of modern industrial society which developed as industrialization spread from the West to Japan and more recently to Korea, Taiwan, Hong Kong, and Singapore. The patterns found here will be examined in the context of the East Asian cultural heritage and late development strategy, to provide new perspective on Western industrial societies.

Foreign Cultures 27. The Novel in East Asia

Examines some of the major works of modern Chinese and Japanese fiction in cultural context, both as distinctive expressions of experience through an imported literary mode and in relation to their own rich narrative traditions. Readings (in translation) will include stories and novels by Lu Hsün, Mao Tun, Sōseki, Tanizaki, and Kawabata.

Note: Meets the requirement in Literature and Arts A.

Foreign Cultures 29. Sub-Saharan African Civilizations

A multidisciplinary introduction to Sub-Saharan African societies, past and present. Selected topics will examine, within a historical context, aspects of African social, economic and political systems, religion, art, and literature. The course will balance social science and humanistic perspectives and relate contemporary patterns to their historical background.

Foreign Cultures 32. Political Doctrines and Society: Modern France

French thought, social structure, and institutions from the Revolution to the end of the 19th century (fall term), and in the 20th century (spring term). French response to social and political problems explained through an analysis of the influence of uniquely French values on common Western political ideas and of the effect of French ideas, patterns of authority, and social behavior upon French politics. Readings from theorists and statesmen such as de Tocqueville, Proudhon, Maurras, Jaurés, Alain, and de Gaulle, and from representative literary figures such as Michelet, Péguy, Camus, Malraux, and Sartre.

Note: Each term may be taken independently. Meets the Core requirement in Foreign Cultures only for students in sections using the native language.

Full course.

Notes

1. A Century of Change

1. Frederick Rudolph, *The American College* (New York: Alfred H. Knopf, 1962), p. 106.

2. Quoted in Samuel Eliot Morison, ed., *The Development of Harvard University, 1869-1929* (Cambridge: Harvard University Press, 1930), p. 558.

3. Eliot's commitment to advanced scholarship developed gradually in the course of his presidency, partly under pressure of competition with the Johns Hopkins University. Hugh Hawkins, *Between Harvard and America: The Educational Leadership of Charles W. Eliot* (New York: Oxford University Press, 1972), p. 65.

4. *President's Annual Report* (1907), pp. 20-24.

5. Seymour M. Lipset and David Riesman, *Education and Politics at Harvard* (New York: McGraw Hill, 1975), p. 129.

6. U.S. Bureau of the Census, *Historical Statistics of the United States* (Washington: Government Printing Office, 1975), I, 379.

7. Barrett Wendell, "Our National Superstition," *North American Review* 179 (1904), 388-401.

8. Greene quoted in Marcia G. Synnott, *The Half-Opened Door: Discrimination and Admissions at Harvard, Yale and Princeton, 1900-1970* (Westport, Conn.: Greenwood Press, 1979), p. 33; Lucien Price, *Dialogues of Alfred North Whitehead* (Boston: Little, Brown, 1954), p. 110; Samuel Eliot Morison, *Three Centuries of Harvard, 1636-1936* (Cambridge: Harvard University Press, 1965), p. 441.

9. Price, *Dialogues of Whitehead*, p. 110.

10. Frederick Rudolph, *Curriculum: A History of the American*

Undergraduate Course of Study since 1636 (San Francisco: Jossey-Bass, 1977), p. 224.

11. Between World Wars I and II there were several imaginative efforts to develop a fresh approach to collegiate education, most notably Alexander Meiklejohn's Experimental College at the University of Wisconsin, which enjoyed a five-year life. Bennington, Sarah Lawrence, and Stevens colleges, inspired by John Dewey, installed curricula based on "life needs"; and Reed College developed the model of an intensive honors seminar program. We are concerned here with more widely influential efforts to sustain general education in a university setting.

12. For a more detailed discussion of the Columbia, Chicago, and Harvard programs, see Daniel Bell, *The Reforming of General Education* (New York: Columbia University Press, 1966), pp. 12-53.

13. *General Education in a Free Society* (Cambridge: Harvard University Press, 1945), pp. 43, 51. The Redbook's authors included four historians (Paul Buck, Wilbur Jordan, Arthur Schlesinger, and Benjamin Wright), two classicists (Raphael Demos and John Finley), two professors of education (Robert Ulich and Philip Rulon), a professor of English (I. A. Richards), and two scientists (Leigh Hoadley and George Wald).

14. This and preceding quotes are from *General Education*, pp. 8, 65, 43, 47, 100.

15. *General Education*, p. 207.

16. Although it was intended that courses in each area would be equivalent—students could not take more than one for college credit —the fact that students were not expected to take the *same* courses set Harvard's program distinctly apart from those at Chicago and Columbia. The reason was partly a matter of size: Harvard College was substantially larger than Chicago or Columbia.

17. By 1976 about 7 percent of American colleges of arts and sciences maintained core general education programs in which students took the same courses or read the same books. Almost 90 percent used a distribution formula, which at one extreme included a few specified courses and at the other extreme was merely recommended rather than required. Approximately 3 percent had no "program" of general education or distribution requirement. Arthur Levine, *Handbook on Undergraduate Curriculum* (San Francisco: Jossey-Bass, 1978), pp. 10-14.

18. Clark Kerr, *The Uses of the University* (Cambridge: Harvard University Press, 1972), pp. 86-88. Illustrating the exponential growth of knowledge, Derek Price points out that in 1750 there were approximately ten scientific journals in the world. Since then, the number has

increased by a factor of ten every half-century. By 1830 no scientist could keep up with the work then published in three hundred journals, so the abstract journal was invented. These, too, multiplied by a factor of ten in every half-century. Thus by 1950 the number of abstract journals "attained a critical magnitude of about three hundred, and scientists began to talk of the need for an abstract of abstracts." Derek Price, *Science since Babylon*, rev. ed. (New Haven: Yale University Press, 1975), pp. 165-168.

As for the growing diversity of knowledge, Daniel Bell cites the listing in the National Register of Scientific and Technical Personnel of "over 900 distinct scientific and technical specializations (outside the social sciences and humanities), compared with 54 listed twenty years ago." The list includes ten basic divisions of physics, seventeen separate fields in the life sciences, eighteen subspecialties in biophysics, seventeen in biochemistry, twenty-six in physical chemistry, seven in geochemistry, thirteen in oceanography. Bell, *Reforming of General Education*, p. 76.

19. Kerr, *Uses of the University*, p. 53.

20. Nathan M. Pusey, *American Higher Education, 1945-1970* (Cambridge: Harvard University Press, 1978), p. 17.

21. Bureau of the Census, *Historical Statistics*, pp. 10 and 382; National Center for Educational Statistics, *Digest of Educational Statistics 1980* (Washington: Government Printing Office, 1980) pp. 8 and 115. In 1940 17 percent of the eighteen-year-old population entered college. By 1960 that proportion rose to 37 percent and in 1970 apparently leveled off at around 46 percent.

22. The growth rate for senior faculty was 21 percent, while that for junior faculty (in the ladder ranks) was 153 percent.

23. Quote is from Laurence R. Veysey, *The Emergence of the American University* (Chicago: University of Chicago Press, 1965), p. 248.

24. When Lowell failed in his overt attempt to restrict the number of Jewish students at Harvard, he introduced new general rules and criteria for selection that had the same effect. Synnott, *Half-Opened Door*, pp. 109-110.

25. According to a report on college admissions policy in 1960: "A four-year mathematics requirement would have kept out of Harvard no fewer than 126 of the 344 students who graduated summa cum laude or magna cum laude in the Classes of 1957 and 1958 . . . The three-year secondary school language requirement would have excluded 127 of the same select group." *Admission to Harvard College: A Report by the Special Committee on College Admissions, February, 1960*, p. 18.

26. W. J. Bender, "Final Report" in *Report of the President of Harvard College and the Reports of Departments, 1959-1960*, pp. 20-21.

27. Ibid., pp. 22, 26-28, 38. McGeorge Bundy, who was dean of faculty during most of Bender's term as head of admissions, later denied that Bender held anti-intellectual prejudices: "What he really had in mind was that even very able boys do not, in America, wish to be *only* intellectuals, so that a college which wants the widest possible choice among the most promising young men must seem to be more than a haven for bookworms." McGeorge Bundy, "Were Those the Days?" *Daedalus* (Summer 1970), 541.

28. These funds helped to reverse the declining proportion of students from low-income families. But as the proportion of students receiving Harvard scholarship grants rose from 26 percent in 1960 to 41 percent in 1980, the median family income of scholarship holders stayed well above the national median.

29. Bender, "Final Report," pp. 11-12. Roughly ten years later, in the midst of campus upheaval, the faculty voted to continue financial support even for those students on probationary status for reasons of conduct or academic performance.

30. *Report of the Special Committee to Review the Present Status and Problems of the General Education Program*, May, 1964.

31. A study conducted at Berkeley showed that between the early 1960s and the early 1970s the percentage of A grades awarded at fifty universities more than doubled, rising from 16 percent to 37 percent. Sidney Suslow, "A Report on an Interinstitutional Survey of Undergraduate Scholastic Grading, 1960s to 1970s," Office of Institutional Research, University of California, Berkeley, February, 1976.

32. Gerald Grant and David Riesman, *The Perpetual Dream: Reform and Experiment in the American College* (Chicago: University of Chicago Press, 1978), p. 179.

33. David Riesman argues that students' demand for curricular reform in the 1960s grew out of accumulated resentment and anxiety over their generation's experience: Sputnik-inspired pressures for academic achievement in high school, the singularly intense competition for places in selective colleges among children of the baby boom and, once in college, the drive to do "harder, more complex, and better work" which "did not bring more reward in terms of a rise in grading during the early and middle 1960s." According to Riesman, this "contrameritocratic" sentiment among the academically successful substantially enlarged the base of support for political protest at Harvard at the end of the decade. Lipset and Riesman, *Education and Politics at Harvard*, pp. 331-332; Grant and Riesman, *Perpetual Dream*, pp. 191-205.

34. Kerr, *Uses of the University*, pp. 136-137.

35. Lawrence E. Eichel, Kenneth W. Jost, Robert D. Luskin, and Richard M. Neustadt, *The Harvard Strike* (Boston: Houghton Mifflin, 1970), p. 48; Lipset and Riesman, *Education and Politics at Harvard*, pp. 217-218.

36. SDS leaflet, April 9, 1969, printed in Eichel et al., *The Harvard Strike*, p. 353.

37. Lipset and Riesman, *Education and Politics at Harvard*, pp. 221-224.

38. Admission to Harvard College was not placed on a sex-blind basis until 1975. Before 1943, women undergraduates were admitted to and graduated from a separate women's college, Radcliffe, where they were housed in single-sex dormitories and instructed by Harvard professors. Subsequently, coeducation replaced the separate system of instruction. Twenty years later, women were awarded Harvard degrees, and by 1971 housing became fully co-residential. One of Derek Bok's first acts as president was to announce that the proportion of women undergraduates would increase from 25 percent to 40 percent, where it remained steady under sex-blind admissions procedures. But it was not until the merger of the two admissions offices in 1975 that women were recruited as widely as men undergraduates and given equal access to the substantially larger scholarship resources of Harvard College.

2. The Search for a Mandate

1. Through the year 1975-1976 the chairmen of the seven task forces met at regular intervals with Rosovsky and his administrative associates to review the progress of each study group. The membership of this "coordinating committee" included Presidents Derek Bok and Matina Horner (Radcliffe College), Professors George Carrier, John Fairbank, Paul Martin, Francis Pipkin, Wilga Rivers, Zeph Stewart, Stephen Williams, and James Q. Wilson, and Deans Phyllis Keller, Edward Wilcox, and Charles Whitlock.

2. More recently Nozick has published a general work of philosophy, *Philosophical Explanations* (Cambridge: Harvard University Press, 1981), whose section on philosophy as part of the humanities (pp. 619-627) was shaped by his thinking about the Core Curriculum.

3. The Wilson version allocated three out of eight required fields to science and mathematics, and the same proportion—three out of eight, or 38 percent—to the humanities. In the Bailyn version it appeared that science and mathematics had been reduced to one out of

five fields, or 20 percent, and the humanities increased to three out of five, or 60 percent.

3. Getting at the Core

1. Similar arguments against permitting students to satisfy Core requirements by examination were made by teachers in all areas. The exam option proposed by the Task Force on the Core Curriculum dropped out of consideration at an early stage.

2. On a later occasion James Q. Wilson argued that changes in the number of Core areas had created "a false issue." He thought that the 1978 version of the Core was "so close to the (1977) Task Force report in almost every respect that it is mildly uncanny. I regard this as evidence that a Core really exists." Letter to P. Keller, November 1981.

4. The Politics of Curricular Reform

1. In March 1978 a small group calling itself Students Against the Core Curriculum (SACC) attempted to rally student support for an official demonstration against the plan. By early April SACC decided to "cancel" the demonstration because "students are not concerned enough about the Core." Another group organized by ten freshmen and calling itself the Ad Hoc Committee on the Core refused to join an organized protest, preferring instead to circulate the petition calling for postponement. Key *Harvard Crimson* reports and commentaries are in the issues dated February 8, 25, March 8, 20, 25, April 10, 11, and May 16, 1978. See also *The Harvard Independent*, February 23 and March 9, 1978.

2. An Andrew W. Mellon Foundation grant eased the transition by funding a small number of new junior faculty appointments in humanities departments hard-pressed by Core commitments. For the most part these positions were used to release senior faculty for Core teaching. But after the grant period, the new positions will be maintained by internal shifting of Harvard resources.

3. The extended discussion of undergraduate education between 1975 and 1978 was not limited to issues raised by the Core proposals. During that period the six task forces appointed by Rosovsky (in addition to the Task Force on the Core Curriculum) consulted widely and reported back—with one exception—to the Faculty Council and/ or to the faculty at large. These reports covered a broad range of issues including admissions policy, concentrations, college life, advising, pedagogical improvement, and the allocation of educational re-

sources. Since they differed considerably in the quality of presentation and analysis, the reports elicited varying degrees of interest. For the most part, they recommended tightening up administrative practices, especially in the area of student advising; monitoring student progress toward the degree; and regular qualitative reviews of departmental courses, concentration requirements, and instructional programs. Several of these recommendations were approved by the faculty; others that did not require faculty action were implemented even before the reports were published. The Task Force on Educational Resources deliberately lagged behind the others to take account of any financial consequences that might flow from their work. But the fiscal problems of the Faculty were changing so rapidly in this period that the Task Force never issued a formal report. Instead, its discussions led Rosovsky to reorganize his administrative staff in order to develop the capacity for long-range financial planning.

4. For a detailed discussion of current admissions policy and practices see Penny H. Feldman, "Recruiting an Elite: Admission to Harvard College," doctoral dissertation, Harvard University, 1975; and Synnott, *Half-Opened Door*, pp. 202-210.

Index

Abernathy, Frederick, 116-117
Academic specialization: and
  general education, 11-12,
  16, 25-26, 40, 49; and diverse
  faculty, 21, 135, 163; and Core
  Curriculum, 51, 53, 68, 123,
  130, 137. *See also* Faculty
Admission standards: under President Eliot, 4, 6, 8; and Jews,
  6, 21, 169n24; and diverse
  student body, 8, 21-24, 41-42,
  44-45, 160-161; raising of, 20,
  21, 23-24; and Core Curriculum, 118, 122-123, 151
Advanced Standing Program,
  24-25, 26
Atlantic Monthly, 3, 141

Bailyn, Bernard, 69-73, 76, 83,
  86, 121-122
Baker, Herschel, 46
Beer, Samuel, 68-69, 130-131
Bell, Daniel, 91
Bender, Wilbur J., 22-23, 24, 48
Berenson, Bernard, 6
Bok, Derek, 34-35, 93, 106, 115,
  122, 155, 158
Bossert, William, 115-116, 120,
  121
Bowersock, Glen W., 106, 111
Briggs, LeBaron Russell, 7

Brooks, Harvey, 76
Brown, Roger, 137

Cambridge University, 2, 3-4, 151
Carrier, George, 65-66, 68, 69, 70
Carter, Jimmy, 143
Caves, Richard, 90-91
Change Magazine, 142-143, 146
Chase, Alston, 141-142
Chicago Tribune, 145
Center for International Affairs,
  20
Center for Middle Eastern Studies,
  19
Central committee, 106-110. *See
  also* Core Curriculum
Clive, John L., 76
Columbia College, 11-12, 15, 16,
  17, 31
Commentary, 142
Committee on Undergraduate
  Education, 111, 126, 152
Computers, 100, 102
Conant, James Bryant, 17, 21,
  23, 43, 48, 96, 160
Coolidge, Archibald Cary, 7
Core Curriculum: goals of, 46,
  48, 54, 62-68, 75, 120, 137,
  141-149; scope of, 56, 99, 107,
  113-114, 121; and curriculum
  areas, 54-56, 63-64, 70-73, 76-

106; administrative structure of, 56-58, 68, 114-115; faculty involvement in, 56-57, 60-63, 76-77, 89, 107, 111, 131-132, 135-139, 149; criticism of, 61-66, 69-73, 115-119, 123, 141-146; and humanists, 61-62, 70-73, 86-90; and scientists, 95-97, 118-119, 138-139, 150, 156; exemptions, 107, 152; student involvement in, 111-112, 139-141, 149; provisions for flexibility of, 112-113, 124-127, 152-153; compared to General Education, 121-122, 137, 142-143, 145, 147-148, 164; and financial considerations, 134-135, 138, 164-165; and social scientists, 142; implementation of, 149-155; course evaluation in, 153-155; evaluation of, 155-158, 164-165. See also Expository Writing; Foreign Cultures; Foreign language requirement; Historical Study; Literature and Arts; Quantitative reasoning requirement; Science; Social Analysis and Moral Reasoning; Task Force on the Core Curriculum
Cornell, Ezra, 3
Cornell University, 3
Course Evaluation Guide, 154
Curriculum, Harvard: before President Eliot, 1-2; under President Eliot, 3-10, 159-161; and elective system, 4-5, 6-7, 17-18, 25-27, 51-53; and college catalogue, 5, 28, 52, 66, 67; under President Lowell, 9-10, 160-161; and concentration-distribution-elective system, 9-11, 16-17, 110, 130-131, 160; and common intellectual purpose, 11, 18, 48, 68, 120, 160, 163; and General Education Program, 14-18, 24-26 (see also General Education); and courses in Western Civilization, 15, 54, 61-62, 72-73, 82, 88-89, 104, 128; and financial considerations, 19-21, 134-135,

164-165; and Freshman Seminar Program, 25-26; and Independent Studies for Ungraded Credit, 26-27; increasing diversity of, 25-29, 32-34, 38-39, 55, 133-134, 159, 162-163; and conflicting social goals, 28-29, 32, 33, 38-39, 134; and Students for a Democratic Society, 30-31. See also Core Curriculum

Dartmouth College, 102
Department of Visual and Environmental Studies, 81
Development Advisory Service, 20
Doty Committee, 17, 25, 70
Dowling, John E., 76

East Asian Research Center, 19
Educational Resources Group (ERG), 111-112, 114, 126
Elective system, 4-10, 51-53, 110, 159; and General Education Program, 17-18, 35
Eliot, Charles William, 1-9, 16, 159-161
Engel, Peter, 142
Enrollment, growth of: high school, 7-8, 14; college, 14, 16, 19, 20, 39
European universities, 2, 3-4, 12, 44
Expository Writing, 54, 73, 83-85, 109, 112

Faculty: specialization of, 12, 21, 28, 135, 142, 163-164; and student rebellion (1968-69), 30-32; and involvement in general education policies, 37-40, 52, 54-55, 135-137; and development of Core Curriculum, 56-57, 60-63, 76-77, 89, 107, 111, 135-139, 149
Faculty Council, 62-63, 69-74, 96-97, 111-114, 124-127
Fanger, Donald L., 76
Foote, Timothy, 145
Ford, Franklin, 46, 47-48
Foreign Cultures, 72-73, 102-106, 107, 108, 112, 147; educational

goals of, 103-104. *See also* Foreign language requirement

Foreign language requirement, 58-61, 62, 71, 73, 105-106, 109, 151

Freshman Seminar Program, 25-26

General Education: and academic specialization, 11-12, 16, 25-26, 40, 49, 53; at Columbia, 11-12; at University of Chicago, 12-13; at Harvard, 14-18, 24-26; and increasing curriculum diversity, 17-18, 25-29, 32-34, 38-39, 55, 133-134; and Advanced Standing, 24, 25; and Freshman Seminar Program, 25-26; and definition of educated person, 41-46, 109-110, 115-116; and Core Curriculum, 48-61 *passim*, 68-69, 72, 121-122, 136-137, 142-148, 164. *See also* Core Curriculum

General Education in a Free Society (Harvard "Redbook"), 14-18, 43

Gilman, Daniel Coit, 3

Gleason, Andrew, 100-101

Graduate School of Arts and Sciences, 15, 35

Graduate schools, 12, 21, 38, 135; and President Eliot, 4, 5, 16

Grant, Gerald, 28

Greene, Jerome D., 9

Harvard College: in nineteenth century, 1-9; compared to European universities, 2, 3-4, 44; under President Eliot, 3-10, 159-160, 161; and elective system, 4-10, 17-18, 35, 51-53, 110, 159; admission standards of, 4, 6, 8, 20-24, 41-45, 160-161; role of faculty at, 5, 37-38, 55 (*see also* Faculty); social goals of, 5-6, 32, 35, 159-162, 164-165; under President Lowell, 9-10, 160; student body of, 9-10, 21-24, 51, 94, 161-162; and General Education Program, 14-18, 24-26 (*see also* General Education); and financial considerations, 19-21, 134-

135, 164-165; and curriculum diversity, 25-29, 34, 55, 159 (*see also* Curriculum); and grading system, 27-28, 170; student rebellions at, 29-33; under Dean Rosovsky, 35-46. *See also* Core Curriculum; Task Force on the Core Curriculum

Harvard Crimson, 52, 89, 124, 139-140

High schools, 6-8, 14, 59; college preparation by, 6, 7-8, 9, 24, 25, 100-101, 162; public and private, 9, 23, 25

Historical Study, 71-72, 107, 121-122, 127, 128-129, 151; educational goals of, 86-90

Hoffmann, Stanley H., 76

Holmes, Oliver Wendell, Jr., 2

Holmes, Oliver Wendell, Sr., 3

Hutchins, Robert Maynard, 12

Jewett, Fred, 122, 151

Johns Hopkins University, 3

Joint Center for Urban Studies, 19

Kaiser, Walter J., 76

Keenan, Edward L., 106

Keller, Phyllis, 46, 106

Kerr, Clark, 18-19, 29, 134

Literature and Arts, 71-72, 77-85, 107, 127, 151; and Expository Writing, 53, 73, 83-85, 109, 112; educational goals of, 77-80, 83; and Fine Arts or Music, 80-81, 147, 156-157; and Contexts of Culture, 81-83

Lowell, Abbott Lawrence, 7, 9-10, 16, 160-161

Lynn, Kenneth, 142, 157

Mackey, George W., 99

Marius, Richard, 83-84, 85

Martin, Paul C., 106, 118, 125

Mill, John Stuart, 53

Morison, Samuel Eliot, 10

Nash, Leonard, 46, 48

Nozick, Robert, 46, 49, 50-51, 128-129; 171

O'Connell, Barry, 143
Oxford University, 2, 3-4, 151

Perkins, Dwight D., 76
Pound, Robert, 46, 48-49, 50-51, 75-76; educational views of, 49, 52-53, 64, 123; faculty response to, 61, 65, 66, 67
Pusey, Nathan, 19-20, 31

Quantitative reasoning requirement, 100-102, 109, 147, 151-152

Redbook, Harvard, 14-18, 43
Reischauer, Edwin, 76
Restic, Joe, 27
Riesman, David, 28
Rosovsky, Henry, 34-46, 105, 134, 157-158, 159; "Letter to the Faculty on Undergraduate Education," 37-40, 136-137; "Undergraduate Education: Defining the Issues," 41-46; educational views of, 42-46, 109, 149; and Task Force report, 60-61, 62, 66, 69, 71; and development of Core areas, 76-77, 99, 114-115; and central planning committee, 106, 110-111; and criticism and amendments of Core Curriculum, 118, 123, 125, 126, 130, 131-132; and faculty involvement, 135-136, 138, 150, 157-158
Rudolph, Frederick, 11
Russian Research Center, 19

St. John's College (Annapolis), 12
Science, 72, 73, 127, 147, 153, 164; educational goals of, 95-99, 118-119, 121; and course development, 150, 156
Shaler, Nathaniel, 7
Simmons, Adele, 145
Skocpol, William, 113
Slive, Seymour, 47
Social Analysis and Moral Reasoning, 72, 90-95, 107, 127, 151; educational goals of, 90-95, 147-148
Solbrig, Otto, 127-128

Standing Committee on the Core program, 149, 152-155
Students for a Democratic Society, 30-31
Students, 66-67, 94, 161-162; riots by, 2, 5; admission standards for diversity of, 8, 21-24, 41-42, 44-45, 160-161; and electives, 9, 51; rebellion by, 29-33; and Core Curriculum, 111-112, 122-123, 139-141, 149

Task Force on the Core Curriculum, 46-73; goals of, 46, 54, 62, 63, 66-68, 75; membership of, 46-49; and required courses, 50-56, 64, 69-70, 71-72, 73-74; report of, 54-61; and Expository Writing, 54, 73; and curriculum areas, 54-56, 63-64, 70-73; and administrative structure, 56-58, 68; and foreign language requirement, 58-61, 62, 71, 73; and humanities, 61-62, 70-73; criticism of, 61-66, 69-73; and Core Curriculum areas, 88-89, 90, 93, 95-97, 100, 102-103. See also Core Curriculum
Task forces on admissions, concentrations, college life, advising, pedagogical improvement, educational resources, 172-173
Thornton, John, 46, 49, 66-67
Time, 145

University Health Service, 58
University of Chicago, 11, 12-13, 16, 17, 145
University of North Carolina, 2

Walzer, Michael, 68, 76, 92, 120-121
Washington Monthly, 142
Wayland, Francis, 2
Wendell, Barrett, 8-9
Westheimer, Frank, 67, 118-119, 121
White, Andrew Dixon, 3
White, Harrison, 116
Whitehead, Alfred North, 10
White House parley on national curricular priorities, 143-144

Whitlock, Charles P., 106
Wilcox, Edward T., 106, 124
Wilson, E. O., 119-120
Wilson, James Q., 106, 127-128, 135, 154, 158; as chairman of Task Force, 46-47, 50; and Task Force report, 51, 54-57, 60-65 *passim*, 69, 70, 71, 73;

"Harvard's Core Curriculum: A View from the Inside," 146-147
Wilson Task Force (Wilson plan), *see* Task Force on the Core Curriculum

Zweng, Nancy, 46, 49, 51, 66